Wallace Stevens: The Making of the Poem

Also by the author:

Stevens' Poetry of Thought, 1966

Wallace Stevens: A Celebration, 1980 (edited with Robert Buttel)

Wallace Stevens

THE MAKING OF THE POEM

 FRANK DOGGETT

The Johns Hopkins University Press : Baltimore and London

Grateful acknowledgment is made to Alfred A. Knopf, Inc., for permission
to quote from the following copyrighted works of Wallace Stevens: *The Collected Poems of Wallace Stevens; Opus Posthumous*, ed. Samuel French
Morse; and *The Palm at the End of the Mind: Selected Poems and a Play*,
ed. Holly Stevens. Acknowledgment is also made to Holly Stevens for permission to quote the Stevens "juvenilia" verses from Robert Buttel, *Wallace
Stevens: The Making of Harmonium* (Princeton: Princeton University Press,
1967). Portions of Chapters 2 and 6 originally appeared as "The Transition
from *Harmonium*: Factors in the Development of Stevens' Later Poetry," in
PMLA 88 (1973): 122–31, and are reprinted by permission of the Modern
Language Association of America. Portions of Chapters 1 and 2 originally
appeared as "Stevens on the Genesis of a Poem" in *Contemporary Literature*
16 (Autumn 1975): 463–77, and are reprinted by permission of the University of Wisconsin Press.

The Johns Hopkins University Press, Baltimore, Maryland 21218
The Johns Hopkins Press Ltd., London
Library of Congress Catalog Number 79-22772
ISBN 0-8018-2324-2
Library of Congress Cataloging in Publication data will be found on the last
printed page of this book.

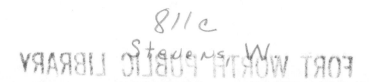

To my wife, Dorothy Emerson

. . . the brooder seeking the acutest end
Of speech: to pierce the heart's residuum
And there to find music for a single line,
Equal to memory, one line in which
The vital music formulates the words.

—Stevens, "Extracts from Addresses to the Academy of Fine Ideas"

Contents

Preface

Wallace Stevens' theories of the nature of creativity and his explanations of poems interspersed with memories of writing them compose a store of materials useful for the illumination of his poetry. Glimpses of the poet writing are richly dispersed throughout certain of his letters, are given here and there in essays, and are even the substance of some poems. His journal shows evidence of a temperament and an aptitude for insight that accord with his unique expressiveness as a poet.

The most interesting hints about the writing of poems and about their meanings, usually offered in elliptical terms, are in Stevens' generous discussions of his work for friends and critics. Often an explanation lapses into a memory of the poem as it existed in meditation before the poem was written, or a memory of the occasion of an initial impulse for a poem. "This occurred to me one late summer afternoon while I was killing time in Washington" explains the origin of "capitol" and "terraces" and "the mighty man," in "Anecdote of Canna" (*L,* 465).[1] "X is the President," he further explained. His casual remarks on the forming of a poem may reveal the restricting human element. For instance, he said that when he was going ahead with a poem, he might use what quickly came to mind so that his impetus would continue. "Anyhow, one is trying to do a poem which may be organized out of whatever material one can snatch up" (*L,* 361).

It is through a study of his theories and memories and through analysis of elements of his artistry and Stevens' disclosures of his creative intuitions that I have hoped to evolve a fresh view of the poetry. Some of Stevens' explanations of his poems are more illuminating than others. Those used here were chosen because they disclose something of his sense of himself in the act of making a poem, or imply something about his idea of the function of meaning, or reveal other aspects of his poetics.

Stevens purposed that a poem's meaning should always be a little beyond determination. "When one wrote on a literal level one was not writing poetry," he affirmed (*L,* 710). That the truth of poetry should be a sense of objective reality and that such a reality could never be known in itself was an ideal that gave his poems the uncertainty he believed they must have to be objects of enduring contemplation. "That a man's work should remain indefinite is often intentional," he wrote Robert Pack (*L,* 863). He considered that meaning in poetry had a function like that of truth in philosophy: to be always desired, to be the always possible and fugitive object of the searching mind.

In the making of his poems, Stevens felt that he was at work with fundamental processes that were, in essence, elemental forces. If his reason was involved, then, as he said, "The reason is a part of nature and is controlled by it" (*OP,* 170). If his creative imagination was offering its flow of invention, he knew that "in the world of words, the imagination is one of the forces of nature" (*OP,* 170). It is with Stevens' contemplations of the "hidden well" of inventiveness within himself that this book begins.

1. See list of abbreviations on p. 2.

Acknowledgments

The work on this book has been in large part the result of a continual discourse on the poetry of Stevens with my wife, Dorothy Emerson. She has contributed both ideas about the poetry and explanations of poems for this book, as well as for my first book, *Stevens' Poetry of Thought*.

I am grateful to the Ingram Merrill Foundation for assistance that enabled me to complete this book. That assistance resulted from encouragement and support given by Robert Buttel, Samuel French Morse, Helen Vendler, and Aubrey Williams. I owe thanks to Holly Stevens for taking me through the rooms and gardens of the Stevens home in Hartford and explaining the place of each in the life of the household. I am also endebted to Peter Brazeau for advice and a guided tour of Hartford, and for a similar experience in Reading given me by John and Edith Douds.

I have read and admired the excellent criticism of Stevens. Especially important to me were *The Clairvoyant Eye*, by Joseph

Riddel; *Wallace Stevens: Poetry as Life*, by Samuel French Morse; *Wallace Stevens: The Making of Harmonium*, by Robert Buttel; *Introspective Voyager*, by A. Walton Litz; *On Extended Wings*, by Helen Vendler; and *Wallace Stevens: The Poems of Our Climate*, by Harold Bloom. I have enjoyed a number of other studies of Stevens, but an extended listing would be of no value to the reader of this book. I should add, however, that Louis Martz's idea of meditation in poetry was a valuable concept for me to hold in mind when I was working on my second chapter. Most important of all was the work of Holly Stevens in editing the *Letters of Wallace Stevens*, in writing and editing *Souvenirs and Prophecies*, and in dating the poems for *The Palm at the End of the Mind*.

Wallace Stevens: The Making of the Poem

Abbreviations

All quotations cited by these abbreviations are by Wallace Stevens.

CP   Wallace Stevens. *The Collected Poems of Wallace Stevens.* New York: Knopf, 1955.

NA   Wallace Stevens. *The Necessary Angel.* New York: Knopf, 1951.

OP   Wallace Stevens. *Opus Posthumous.* New York: Knopf, 1957.

L   Holly Stevens, ed. *Letters of Wallace Stevens.* New York: Knopf, 1966.

Buttel   Robert Buttel. *Wallace Stevens: The Making of Harmonium.* Princeton: Princeton University Press, 1967.

PEM   Holly Stevens, ed. *The Palm at the End of the Mind.* New York, Vintage Books, 1972.

WS   Frank Doggett and Robert Buttel, eds. *Wallace Stevens: A Celebration.* Princeton: Princeton University Press, 1980.

One

THE VOICE, THE BOOK,
THE HIDDEN WELL

I

Even as a young poet, Wallace Stevens spoke of poetry as something given as well as made. "I am full of bright threads," he wrote in his journal for July 24, 1899, referring, it would seem, to unbidden elements: sudden phrases, floating images, floating thoughts. Then, with a wish that he could bring his conscious will to bear upon what chance brought to mind, he added, "if I could only gather them together" (*L*, 30). Ten years later, with a similar sense of a distinction between the will of the artist and what was within him but not controlled by him, he looked for the creative source—"looked into myself and found everything covered up" (*L*, 120). By the time he was writing "The Comedian as the Letter C," he had begun to conceive of two origins for poetry—the "wakefulness" that is the conscious, shaping intelligence and the "meditating sleep" that is unconscious inventiveness:

That wakefulness or meditating sleep,
In which the sulky strophes willingly
Bore up, in time, the somnolent, deep songs.   (*CP,* 33)

In his maturity and during the period of close examination of his poems and his motives (in the 1930s), Stevens began to wonder if there were a truly volitional factor in creativity. "Perhaps there is no such thing as free will in poetry," he surmised (*L,* 319). When he remembered his own experience of writing a poem, he found it difficult to tell what was planned and what was fortuitous. Choice was an act that seemed to be essentially intentional, yet the discrimination, the taste that during composition became his style, could be considered an event that happened within him, below reason and will. "When we speak of fluctuations of taste, we are speaking of evidences of the operation of the irrational" (*OP,* 229). And later he said, "A man has no choice about his style" (*OP,* 210). If the poet writes what he likes, and what he likes is determined by his individuality, is all this only an accident of the course of things?

It cannot matter at all.
Happens to like is one
Of the ways things happen to fall.   (*OP,* 40)

About the time these lines from "Table Talk" were written, Stevens' letters indicated an interest in determinism. "A most attractive idea to me," he wrote in 1935, "is the idea that we are all the merest biological mechanisms" (*L,* 294). And when he considered "whether a poem about a natural object is roused by the natural object or whether the natural object is clothed with its poetic characteristics by the poet," he decided that he shared the point of view of the boy who, when told to stop sneezing, replied, "I am not sneezing; it's sneezing me" (*L,* 302). Yet, concurrently, when he wrote "The Man with the Blue Guitar," Stevens was the conscious artist, he said, who accomplished his intent with painstaking care. "This is contrary to my usual experience, which is to allow a thing to fill me up and then express it in the most slap-dash way" (*L*, 316).

The year before (1936) he had gathered his ideas about the voluntary and involuntary aspects of creative work into a lecture, "The Irrational Element in Poetry." According to the lecture, selection of a subject is made as much by chance as by choice; development occurs that could not have been planned; fluctuations of taste or of interest subvert the intent of the poet. The rational is the predictable, the willed; the irrational is the fortuitous, the unbidden. As an example, Stevens described an experience of hearing one night a cat walking over the crust of snow beneath his window: "The faintness and strangeness of the sound made on me one of those impressions which one so often seizes as pretexts for poetry" (*OP*, 217). This impression was unpredictable, he concluded, and therefore the source of feeling in the poem, if one were written, would be irrational.

The irrational in Stevens' view is whatever is involuntary, like the force of circumstance, the compulsion of inevitability. The innate character of the poet, for instance, determines the character of his poetry, and the nature of his thought and feeling of the moment forms the poem he is writing. The deterministic bias of Stevens' thinking becomes evident with this notion of the inevitability of a poem's course of development. "If each of us," he says, "is a biological mechanism, each poet is a poetic mechanism." As preface to this extreme position, he tells how he happened to write "The Old Woman and the Statue" and maintains that the poem "has an automatic aspect in the sense that it is what I wanted it to be without knowing before it was written what I wanted it to be, even though I knew before it was written what I wanted to do" (*OP*, 219–20).

This memory of writing a poem and finding what he could not have expected resembles the symbolic reading of the book of unfolding experience in "Phosphor Reading by His Own Light":

> It is difficult to read. The page is dark.
> Yet he knows what it is that he expects.
>
> . . . .
>
> Look, realist, not knowing what you expect.   (*CP*, 267)

To anticipate, and to find one's anticipation surprised as well as fulfilled, is part of the experience of writing, just as it is of reading. By his own account, Stevens, when writing a poem, had at times a feeling of reading it in a book. "Often when I am writing poetry," he says in a letter to Barbara Church, "I have in mind an image of reading a page of a large book: I mean the large page of a book. What I read is what I like" (*L*, 642). Not only did he write what he liked as though already given in a book, but the form, the rhythm, the sound were also come upon as though in "an unwritten rhetoric that is always changing and to which the poet must always be turning. That is the book in which he learns that the desire for literature is the desire for life" (*OP*, 226–27). The book the poet reads subliminally is thus the book of emerging language and, simultaneously, the book of an emerging flow of consciousness. The flow of consciousness is revealed as though read by the subjective principle:

> The thinker as reader reads what has been written.
> He wears the words he reads to look upon
> Within his being.   (*CP*, 492)

II

When he was writing his last few poems, Stevens mentioned "the feelings, the great source of poetry" (*L*, 842). Apparently he usually wrote with ardor, for he told Hi Simons that "poetry is a passion, not a habit" (*L*, 364). Stevens' emotional involvement in composition is disclosed by repeated references to the working poet's intensity of feeling. In "The Figure of the Youth as Virile Poet," he describes that intensity as "the moment of exaltation" (*NA,* 53) and, again, as the "exhilaration that appears to be inseparable from genuine poetic activity" (*NA,* 58). While writing a poem, the poet knows "the pleasure of powers that create a truth that cannot be arrived at by the reason alone" (*NA,* 58). The experience of the poet, he says, is no less than that of the mystic. Under the influence of "aspiration and inspiration," a poet may reach an elevation of feeling that liberates his creative faculties. "In this state of elevation we feel perfectly adapted to the idea that moves and *l'oiseau qui chante*" (*NA,* 51).

"L'oiseau qui chante," like the singing bird of the English romantic poets, seems to be an image of a spontaneous creative act. The image began to accumulate connotations of this kind as early as "Meditation Celestial & Terrestrial," where bird songs celebrate the return of the creative season of the human spirit. In the poem, reason and will are identified with winter and its "narrow sky" of limited human possibility, as compared to warblings of birds associated with the exuberance and fecundity of summer, the drunken or irrational mother:

> But what are radiant reason and radiant will
> To warblings early in the hilarious trees
> Of summer, the drunken mother?   (*CP,* 124)

The singing bird as an image of unconscious creativity is implied by the warblings that come to the poet of "Esthétique du Mal," II. As he lies on a balcony, he hears in the night the sounds of a bird, and these sounds begin to form into a poem on his intuition of that "mal," that essential fault touching everything:

> . . . Warblings became
> Too dark, too far, too much the accents of
> Afflicted sleep, too much the syllables

That would form themselves, in time, and communicate
The intelligence of his despair, express
What meditation never quite achieved.   (*CP*, 314)

The darkness, the remoteness, the sounds of the troubled sleep used to characterize birdsong indicate that the warblings symbolize a creative impulse of the unconscious. When the warblings become syllables and the syllables arrange themselves into language that expresses "what meditation never quite achieved," the involuntary creative powers are at work. The poem that comes to the poet in this way, while he is under the influence of night and the moon (symbols, respectively, of the unconscious and the creative imagination), is "a kind of elegy he found in space." Night and the moon, the poem reveals, are free of the poet, evade his mind as the involuntary imagination always evades conscious meditation.

The moon is a singing bird in "God is Good. It is a Beautiful Night" and symbolizes the creative imagination. The moon is addressed as "brown bird," and its song is the light falling from its fiery wings. High above the individual poet—"the head and zither / On the ground"—it is apart from time and human process, like Keats' immortal bird, and thus seems to stand for the creative imagination of all poets. By the light of this moon that is also the song of the brown bird, the poet creates his poem: "In your light, the head is speaking. It reads the book" (*CP*, 285). Again, writing a poem is like reading a book.

"The Creations of Sound" is another celebration of impromptu invention. Just as song issues spontaneously from the bird, the poetry that is sound issues from the walls, the ceiling, and in the last stanza from the floor, to suggest a source other than the conscious will of the poet:

So that it came to him of its own,
Without understanding, out of the wall

Or in the ceiling, in sounds not chosen,
Or chosen quickly, in a freedom
That was their element.   (*CP*, 310)

The praise of spontaneous creativity in "The Creations of Sound" reflects the poet's pleasure in improvisation. The freedom that is the element in which spontaneity exists is a condition of receptivity "without understanding." The words, the sounds that come to the poet of their own or out of the wall or ceiling are judged intuitively—"chosen quickly," according to the poem. "You have somehow to know the sound that is the exact sound; and you do in fact know, without knowing how," Stevens says of the intuitive judgment of the poet. And then he adds that "what is true of sounds is true of everything: the feeling for words, without regard to their sound, for example" (*OP*, 226).

Stevens had a predilection for ready and fluent creativity and preferred the poems that came to him easily: "I almost always dislike anything that I do that doesn't fly in the window" (*L*, 505). Even the great long poems were written with incredible swiftness, considering the short span of time he could spare for them from his daily life of work. In fact, it was easier for him to keep the momentum of a long poem than to begin over and over with brief ones. In a long poem, "one goes ahead pretty much as one talks, as one thing leads to another" (*L*, 648). Creative work that continues on like talk must be, in some measure, improvisation. Whether largely improvised or carefully wrought, it is amazing that "Esthétique du Mal" was conceived, composed, and completed in six weeks—and all this accomplished outside of long business hours. No wonder, Stevens says of his poems, "these come very easy or not at all" (*L*, 594).[1]

1. In 1913, Stevens said of his poems, "It's a deuce of a job (for me) to do them" (*L*, 180). This was a time before he had achieved the mastery of style that enabled him to write with comparative ease. While he was still working

III

Improvisation seems to be the work of involuntary creative faculties, for it appears in language that is unbidden and unexpected. Emerging from the unknown, the improvised is suddenly part of the known. In "The Irrational Element in Poetry," Stevens says the unknown is to the known as the irrational is to the rational. The remark suggests that he is thinking of the unconscious and the consciousness, especially since he refers to the surrealists (*OP*, 227–28). His statement that the unknown is both the source of what is known and part of the dynamics of the known conforms to his notion that the unconscious "is the beginning and end of the conscious" (*L*, 373). Stevens illustrates his conception of the known and the unknown by an image of light and dark, which also seems to be a visual idea of the conscious as a bright foreground of the dark unconscious: "The rational mind, dealing with the known, expects to find it glistening in a familiar ether. What it really finds is the unknown always behind and beyond the known, giving it the appearance, at best, of chiaroscuro" (*OP*, 228).

As early as 1909, Stevens spoke of the unconscious as the unknown in a fanciful letter on the idea of music. Chords of music, Stevens speculated, "vibrate on more than the 'sensual ear'— vibrate on the unknown." For the unknown, Stevens seems to have had in mind at this time a subliminal racial memory: "It is considered that music, stirring something within us, stirs the Memory. I do not mean our personal Memory—the memory of our twenty years and more—but our inherited Memory, the

---

on "The Man with the Blue Guitar," he said that the poems of that series were often a task for him. "Apparently, only the ones over which I take a great deal of trouble come through finally. This is contrary to my usual experience" (*L*, 316). Later he said that two poems of "Notes toward a Supreme Fiction,"—"Not to be realized" and the poem on the blue woman— were difficult to do (*L*, 434, 463). However, the entire "Notes toward a Supreme Fiction" was written in four months.

Memory we have derived from those who lived before us in our own race, and in other races, illimitable, in which we resume the whole past life of the world, all the emotions, passions, experiences of the millions and millions of men and women now dead, whose lives have insensibly passed into our own, and compose them.—It is a Memory deep in the mind, without images" (*L,* 136). He added that this idea of an "infinite extension of personality" had always been a part of his thinking (*L,* 136).

Many years later, this "extension of personality" becomes the "subman" of "Sombre Figuration," the unconscious presented as another self lying below the conscious self, a child of the antiquity of man who retains in his darkness the collective experience of humanity:

> A self of parents who have never died,
> Whose lives return, simply, upon our lips.　　　　　(*OP,* 67)

The subman, like "the extension of personality" in the letter of 1909, lives in obscure memories:

> Inhabitant, in less than shape, of shapes
> That are dissembled in vague memory.　　　　　(*OP,* 67)

And also, like the unconscious collective memory of that letter, the subman lets us hear music with a subliminal ear, so that we are an audience for "instruments discerned/In the beat of the blood." A Stevens letter explaining this poem revives the concept of a collective unconscious memory set forth thirty-one years earlier: "The future must bear within it every past, not least the pasts that have become submerged in the sub-conscious, things in the experience of races" (*L,* 373).

Collective experience takes the form of a flight of images like a storm of leaves through the mind of the subman. These images, the poem says in its conclusion, are "emblemata" or "thoughts by descent" from the past. The flow of emblemata in the uncon-

scious suggests the idea of archetypal imagery. An echo of this
notion of "thoughts by descent" appears ten years later in "Sketch
of the Ultimate Politician":

> There is a storm much like the crying of the wind,
> Words that come out of us like words within,
> That have rankled for many lives and made no sound.
>
> (CP, 336)

Images that are emblemata and thoughts by descent appear
again as the symbolic shapes made by "a vast people old in meditation" in a poem with the ironic title, "A Completely New Set
of Objects."[2] The poem begins with the concept of a flow or
river ("a Schuylkill") from the unconscious, deep within the
body ("in mid-earth") bearing the emblemata, the symbols of a
collective human memory:

> Things made by mid-terrestrial, mid-human
> Makers without knowing, or intending, uses.   (CP, 352)

This poem, read with the letter of 1909 at hand, is evidence of
the long consistency in the work of Stevens of such concepts as
this one of a collective unconscious memory. The flotillas of
emerging unconsciousness are borne up from antiquity like canoes
paddled by "figures verdant with time's buried verdure." And the
shapes, the archetypes, brought in these flotillas "were the exactest
shaping/Of a vast people old in meditation." This line suggests

---

2. Samuel French Morse found that this poem was "written about the
annual festival on the Schuylkill River 'down which paraded canoes and
boats lighted at night with candled Chinese lanterns,' which he remembered
from his boyhood." See Morse, *Wallace Stevens: Poetry as Life* (New York:
Pegasus, 1970), p. 205. Appropriate to a biographical study, this comment
on the poem is a valuable indication of the source of the imagery rather an
explication of the poem. The poem, however, can be read in symbolic as well
as biographical terms.

the idea of the collective memory that "we have derived," as the 1909 letter says, "from those who lived before us in our own race, and in other races, illimitable." And "the figures verdant with time's buried verdure" resemble shadowy forms, as in the letter on the unconscious memory: "the flitting forms that are its shadowy substance." In the poem, these figures carry with them into the present the symbolic shapes made in ages past:

> Carrying such shapes, of such alleviation,
> That the beholder knew their subtle purpose.　　　(*CP*, 353)

The alleviating shapes, the archetypes, assume traditional form and significance in "Things of August," VIII. Here there is no mention of a buried racial memory, yet it is "the sense of the archaic" that evokes figures like that of "the archaic form/Of a woman with a cloud on her shoulder" or other outlines of common human experience: "the wanderer,/The father, the ancestor, the bearded peer":

> The forgetful color of the autumn day
> Was full of these archaic forms, giants
> Of sense, evoking one thing in many men.　　　(*CP*, 494)

Among these images of universal significance, "giants/Of sense," the male and female archetypes appear to be related to innate feelings about the twofold nature of mind. The mythological form of consciousness in the poetry of Stevens is the bearded face, and its dark unknown base, the unconsciousness of man and nature, is seen as the female figure. Accordingly, day and sun are usually associated with the male figure and night and moon with the female figure. In some poems, the female archetype is patently identified with the creative impulse. "The Candle a Saint," for instance, is a celebration of the creative unconscious personified by Nox, the goddess from whom, in one version of the cosmogenic myth, all things have their origin. Nox, or night, is characterized as green in this poem, to indicate the fecundity of the unconscious. "Green kindled and apparelled," night rises above the human individual, for whom she is the source of inspiration and intuition as "the abstract, the archaic queen" (*CP*, 223).

Symbolic description of consciousness and the unconscious as day and night is part of Stevens' fund of recurring imagery. "Night is the nature of man's interior world," Stevens says of the unconscious in "A Word with José Rodríguez-Feo." The poem concludes with a version of the day-night symbolism, implying that consciousness of reality has its genesis in the unconscious. The point of the poem is, Stevens says, that "although the grotesque has taken possession of the sub-conscious, this is not because there is any particular relationship between the two things" (*L*, 489). The grotesque is what we see:

> . . . It is
> Not apparition but appearance, part
> Of that simplified geography, in which
> The sun comes up like news from Africa.   (*CP*, 334)

The sun rising from Africa and from night is an image of what has just become known to consciousness—its news, rising from the vast subcontinent of the unconscious. Africa was conceived as the unknown and the unconscious long before by Jean-Paul Richter: "The unconscious is really the largest realm in our own minds, and just on account of this unconsciousness the inner Africa, whose unknown boundaries may extend far away."[3]

IV

The word *imagination* is used in many senses in the essays and

---

3. Quoted in Lancelot Law Whyte, *The Unconscious before Freud* (London: Tavistock, 1967), p. 133.

letters of Stevens. For instance, there is an explicatory letter on "Sombre Figuration" that presents two diverse notions of the word: "In another note I said that the imagination partakes of the conscious. Here it is treated as an activity of the sub-conscious: the imagination is the sub-conscious" (*L*, 373). Stevens has in mind here, it seems, two kinds of imagination: the voluntary, which "partakes of the conscious," and the involuntary, which is an activity of the subconscious. Eight years later, in a well-known passage from "Effects of Analogy," Stevens described ideas of the creative faculty that carry further the earlier notion of the dual nature of the imagination. "The poet is constantly concerned with two theories," he says, and goes on to describe the way each one deals with the problem of the poet's grasp of reality. One of these theories holds that the poet practices his art "in the very center of consciousness" (*NA*, 115). When concerned with this theory, Stevens identifies creativity with the intelligence and maintains that the poet works by means of his conscious will. "The poet does his job by virtue of an effort of the mind," Stevens says in another essay, but he is still influenced by this notion of the creative imagination (*NA*, 165).

The other of the two theories considers that the poet's imagination "is not wholly his own but that it may be part of a much larger, much more potent imagination." The idea that it is "not wholly his own" and thus is involuntary, that it has a source larger than consciousness, indicates that the more potent imagination is an activity of the unconscious.[4] It is the poet's business,

4. In accord with this notion of "a much larger, much more potent imagination" is the statement in the letter on "Sombre Figuration" that "the conscious is a lesser thing than the sub-conscious" (*L*, 373). In another letter in explication of a poem, Stevens says "the imagination creates nothing. In short, the subconscious creates nothing" (*L*, 465). What he means is that it (the imagination or the subconscious) creates nothing except what is derived from reality.

Stevens continues, to try to get at this kind of imagination. To do so, he must live or try to live "on the verge of consciousness."

"The verge of consciousness" is also the edge of the unconscious. In the seventh poem of "Notes toward a Supreme Fiction," Stevens designates the edge of the unconscious as "the edge of sleep." Sometimes the edge of the unconscious induces a state of creative facility, the poem explains:

> Perhaps there are moments of awakening,
> Extreme, fortuitous, personal, in which
>
> We more than awaken, sit on the edge of sleep.   (*CP,* 386)

That Stevens had two theories of the creative imagination, one that it was conscious and purposeful, the other that it was unconscious and involuntary, was typical of his mode of thinking. Usually, concepts in Stevens' mind grew binately. His predilection for antithesis can be seen in many poems—"New England Verses," for instance. "Two things of opposite natures seem to depend," he says, "on one another." The germinating idea of this poem from "Notes toward a Supreme Fiction" can be found in a letter to Hi Simons written a little more than a year and a half earlier: "When I was a boy I used to think that things progressed by contrasts, that there was a law of contrasts. But this was building the world out of blocks. Afterwards I came to think more of the energizing that comes from mere interplay, interaction. Thus, the various faculties of the mind co-exist and interact, and there is as much delight in this mere co-existence as a man and a woman find in each other's company" (*L,* 368). Two of the things of opposite nature that coexist and interact within his own person— that is, two "faculties of the mind"—are the two kinds of imagination that find as much delight in their coexistence "as a man and a woman find in each other's company":

Follow after, O my companion, my fellow, my self,
Sister and solace, brother and delight.   (*CP*, 392)

If in these lines Stevens makes his customary assignment of female and male roles for the two selves of one person, the anima
figure of "sister and solace" would represent the unconscious
and "brother and delight" the consciousness.

The idea of two selves in one person occurs in a number of
poems. For instance, there is the "I" as the rational, conscious
self of "Anecdote of the Prince of Peacocks," and there is Ber-
serk, the irrational, the unconscious, who resembles a consciousness in his subtle activity but lives in the somnolence of the
natural world—"As if awake/In the midst of sleep" (*CP*, 58).
Another example of personification of the consciousness and the
unconscious is in "The Virgin Carrying a Lantern" (*CP*, 71). The
virgin is the consciousness fulfilling its conventional roles by the
light of its intelligence, its lantern. This amusing poem pretends
to take the point of view of the social conventions. "There are no
bears among the roses," the poem begins, seeing instead of an
animal the hidden libido among the flowers of sentiment. It is,
the poem continues, a Negress, a dark figure representing the unconscious, who supposes, in the ironic statement of the poem,
"Things false and wrong/About the lantern of the beauty." But
the unconscious is a realist and knows the subliminal erotic life
beneath the pieties and traditional obligations of the roles taken
by the consciousness:

The pity that her pious egress
Should fill the vigil of a negress
With heat so strong!   (*CP*, 71)

In "The Hand as a Being," two selves within one person (the
consciousness and the unconscious) are cast as lover and beloved

to symbolize the latent erotic idea of creativity. The "naked, nameless dame" (the creative unconscious) holds up her hand, symbol of the creative act, to give the man "too conscious of too many things at once" the composure of one released from personal absorption, from the concerns of consciousness:

> Her hand composed him like a hand appeared,
> Of an impersonal gesture, a stranger's hand.   (*CP*, 271)

The idea that the creative act is the work of a stranger's hand, of a second self from whom arises the language that is given, the poem that is read in the unconscious before it is written by the intelligence: this is one of the themes of "The Creations of Sound." If writing a poem is like reading a book—"the large page of a book," as he says in the letter of 1949 to Barbara Church—the words that come to the poet must be those given on that large page. According to "The Creations of Sound," it is better to think that the poem is independent of ego consciousness:

> Better without an author, without a poet,
>
> Or having a separate author, a different poet,
> An accretion from ourselves, intelligent
> Beyond intelligence, an artificial man
>
> At a distance, a secondary expositor,
> A being of sound, whom one does not approach
> Through any exaggeration. From him, we collect.
>
> (*CP*, 310–11)

In "The Creations of Sound," Stevens is concerned almost entirely with the theory of the involuntary imagination. Many contradictory statements of his about the source of poetry can be considered as emanating from a bias for one or the other conception of the nature of creativity, as when he wrote Latimer that "writing poetry is a conscious activity. While poems may very well occur, they had very much better be caused" (*L*, 274).[5] The final stanza of "The Creations of Sound" denies the validity of this kind of exclusion of involuntary creativity:

> We do not say ourselves like that in poems.
> We say ourselves in syllables that rise
> From the floor, rising in speech we do not speak.   (*CP*, 311)

5. This theory of the creative imagination has attracted the attention of some of the best thinking on Stevens; see, for instance, Northrop Frye, "Wallace Stevens and the Variation Form," in *Literary Theory and Structure: Essays in Honor of William K. Wimsatt*, ed. Frank Brady, John Palmer, and Martin Price (New Haven: Yale University Press, 1973), p. 398. See also Louis L. Martz, "Wallace Stevens: The World as Meditation," in *Wallace Stevens*, ed. Marie Borroff (Englewood Cliffs, N.J.: Prentice-Hall, 1963), p. 148.

The essay that seems to substantiate this view is "The Relations between Poetry and Painting"; there Stevens says that "if one questions the dogma that the origins of poetry are to be found in the sensibility and if one says that a fortunate poem or a fortunate painting is a synthesis of exceptional concentration (that degree of concentration that has a lucidity of its own, in which we see clearly what we want to do and do it instantly and perfectly), we find that the operative force within us does not, in fact, seem to be the sensibility, that is to say, the feelings" (*NA*, 164). But Stevens adds that "I have spoken of questioning, not of denying." As Stevens goes on to describe it, the "operative force within us" seems to be distinguishable from conscious will. Of the work of this "constructive faculty" with experience, he says that "what it really does is to use it as material with which it does whatever it wills." Here the "it" that wills seems to be other than the "I" that wills.

The spontaneous imagination of unbidden creative acts that Stevens associates with night or unconscious creativity should not be confused with his derogation of "the false imagination" in the essay "The Figure of the Youth as Virile Poet." There, in his usual role of skeptic, he belittles mystical ideas of the imagination—"the false conception of the imagination as some incalculable *vates* within us, unhappy Rodomontade" (*NA*, 61). To destroy "the false conception of the imagination," one's philosophy must be naturalism, with its firm commitment to the reality about us, to the belief "that the visible is the equivalent of the invisible."

And when dominated by his deterministic bias, he could deny that poems are ever caused and assert that they only occur: "There is more than the romantic in the statement that the true work of art, whatever it may be, is not the work of the individual artist. It is time and it is place, as these perfect themselves" (*NA*, 139–40).

Two

THE MAKER OF A THING
YET TO BE MADE

I

There is an account of the inception of a poem scattered among the comparisons of the creative work of poets and philosophers in the final section of "A Collect of Philosophy" (*OP*, 196–98). There Stevens describes the poet as open to an organizing factor that, if found, may be the seed of a poem—an "integration," he calls it. "Up to the point at which he has found his subject," Stevens says of the poet's passivity to an irruption from the unconscious, "the state of vague receptivity in which he goes about resembles one part of something that is dependent on another part, which he is not quite able to specify." The consciousness is never able to realize, "to specify," the activity of the creative unconscious. However, consciousness is not entirely passive, for it habitually searches for an organization of thought or feeling.

This integration might be a concept or perhaps something less than idea, but it must have some specific imaginative quality that makes it appropriate for the work of the poet. When found, the integration lies at an emotional level of such intensity that "it is not always easy to say whether one is thinking or feeling or doing both at the same time." The poet then experiences "miraculous shortenings of mental processes." The unconscious has been at work, and suddenly "the gist of a poem comes into the poet's mind and takes possession of it."

In one of several versions of the last section of "A Collect of Philosophy," Stevens reveals his appreciation of the importance to his own work of spontaneous creativity. "The poet, in moments of exceptional concentration, sometimes experiences an automatism in which the poem writes itself" (*WS*, 51). In the next sentence, he speaks of the imagination as though it were a kind of creative unconscious, a sense that the word sometimes assumes for him. "It seems as if the imagination realized its intention, however obscure its intention may have been, with an instantaneous directness." It can be inferred from this statement, and from the sentence that follows, that Stevens felt the imagination, in its role of a subliminal inventiveness, acted apart from and independent of the conscious will. "The obscurity of the intentions of the imagination, (the source of poetic urgings), and the accomplishing of the imagination's will by miraculous shortenings of mental process cannot be very different, in poets, from the obscurity of the intentions of the reason (if that really is the source of philosophic urgings), and the accomplishing of the reason's will by miraculous accelerations, in philosophers."

Stevens' lifelong interest in the unconscious and the fortuitous as sources of inceptions, especially those of poems, in no sense obviates his dependence on the work of the intelligence in the making of poems. When his subject enters the center of consciousness, then the poet is the maker; he meditates the idea and shaping of his poem as carefully as a philosopher the logic of his thought. Before this point, Stevens says, the poet's "probing" for a subject is fortuitous. "I am speaking of the time before he has found his subject, because, once he has found his subject, that is to say, once he has achieved the integration for which he has been probing, he becomes as deliberate, in his own way, as the philosopher" (*OP*, 197).

At one time, Stevens was on the verge of beginning a poem but was not sure of what he was going to write. As he told Henry Church, "I am about to settle down to my subject: DESCRIPTION WITHOUT PLACE." At this point, he had found a subject and was not certain that it would be a sufficiently formative concept. "Although this is the second or third subject that I have had in mind, unless it develops quickly and easily as I go along, I may change it" (*L*, 494). This was the moment when it seemed that the operative integration had been found. As he said of estimating the quality of an integration for the making of a poem, "the poet intends his to be effective" (*OP*, 197). If it were, then he could expect "miraculous shortenings of mental processes." Unless it developed "quickly and easily," to use the terminology of the letter, he would know that he had not found his subject (*L*, 494). If he had, then "the gist of a poem" would take possession of his mind, according to the description of the creative process in the essay.

Apparently, considerable intellectual activity occurred after Stevens gained a realization of an idea for a poem. "Ideas of real force don't occur to one every day," he said. "Besides, I want my poetry to grow out of something more important than my inkwell" (*L*, 329). An idea as he thought of it seemed to him to have its own almost organic development: "It is curious how a subject once chosen grows like a beanstalk until it seems as if there had never been anything else in the world" (*L*, 544). In this case, the idea that grew like a beanstalk became an essay, yet the same kind of engendering may be assumed for poems.

Although Stevens indicated in "A Collect of Philosophy" that the search for a poem was a search for an idea, yet elsewhere he said that "in poetry the language is everything" (*L*, 481). The integration itself, he explained in "Two or Three Ideas," was inextricably involved with style: "The effective integration is not a disengaging of the subject. It is a question of the style in which the subject is presented" (*OP*, 204). Stevens' idea that the style of a poem and the poem are one (*OP*, 202) ensured that the integration growing into a poem would develop with an intensity or peculiarity of language inherent in the thinking of the poet at the time. A feeling for the preeminence of style and the belief that style should be constantly enlarged encouraged verbal audacity: "If a poem seems to require a hierophantic phrase, the phrase should pass. This is a way of saying that one of the consequences of the ordination of style is not to limit it, but to enlarge it, not to impoverish it, but to enrich and liberate it" (*OP*, 205).

Stevens' genius for felicity of language also involved the poet's critical intelligence in selection, variation, or even obliquity—all the decisions he must make on his faith in himself alone, like the decision that analysis and evaluation must end: "You examine what you do as you go along, and you examine it afterwards, yet there is a point at which you are bound to stop" (*L*, 500).

II

As early as 1909, Stevens realized a need for a formative element within him that would make expression possible. "There is a great sleepy jumble in me seeking to be arranged, to be set in order, and then to be spoken" (*L*, 115). And years later, he indicated, in "A Collect of Philosophy," that when he found some formative element, an integration might occur that would set in order his random thinking and then initiate a creative process, the end of which would be a poem (*OP*, 196–97).

Relics of Stevens' continuing desire for creative impetus can be discerned in the lists of ideas and images and the notes of impressions found among his miscellaneous papers (*OP*, xxxi–xxxvi). Even the jottings of abandoned titles seem to have been part of this sifting of potential beginnings. "Very often the title occurs to me before anything else occurs to me," he wrote the editor of *Ideas of Order* (*L*, 297). Similarly, just two years before his death, he mentioned a "Hymn to J. Zeller," a poem that was never more than its title, and suggested that a title must hold by implication an idea of generative force for a poem to develop from it. "One is constantly interested in things of that kind which come to nothing. With many, if they are to be realized it must be by their own force." Then, in character with his other statements referring to the ease with which he wrote, he said, "I do not force myself" (*L*, 792).

Elsewhere, he explained that if an integration was to become realized as poetry, it had to have an inherent quality of some kind: "The poet searches for an integration that shall be not so much sufficient in itself as sufficient for some quality that it possesses, such as its insight, its evocative power or its appearance in the eye of the imagination" (*OP*, 196–97). Before he had written any of "Description without Place"—or even determined upon that particular idea rather than another—he had in mind several integrations, one of which was implied by the title of the poem he finally wrote. "It seems to me to be an interesting idea: that is to say, the idea that we live in the description of a place and not in the place itself." Then, indicating that the quality he felt in his title, "Description without Place," was its insight, he added: "and in every vital sense we do" (*L*, 494).

Apparently, Stevens thought of an integration as a conceptual unity, for, in introducing his theory of the genesis of a poem, he said that "the habit of forming concepts is a habit of the mind by which it probes for an integration" (*OP*, 196). When he revealed the source of a poem that was manifestly a concept, it was often one so slight that its special quality for him must have been its evocative force, a suggestiveness that would lead him to additional integrations. For instance, a sense of the flux of opinion was the germinating seed of "Extracts from Addresses to the Academy of Fine Ideas." He noted that "one of the characteristics of the world today is the Lightness with which ideas are asserted, held, abandoned, etc. That is what this poem grows out of" (*L*, 380). The poem modifies the notion with these words:

> The law of chaos is the law of ideas,
> Of improvisations and seasons of belief.   (*CP*, 255)

What he described as the source of the poem led him to formulate the discourse of section V, with its account of ideas as assassins that kill each other, and section III could have developed as an off-shoot of the original integration.

Although Stevens wrote of "probing for an integration" as though poems evolved primarily from concepts, he also mentioned other kinds of sources for poetry—in one case a proclivity in his own subliminal life. "The Westwardness of Everything" must have been realized, he suggested, from his personal tendency for westward orientation. "The house in which I was born and lived as boy faced the west and wherever I have lived if the house faced any other way I have always been pulling it round on an axis to get it straight" (*L*, 618). This predisposition is described in "The Westwardness of Everything" as a "habit of the mind." And to transform this felt impulse into terms for the discourse of a poem, the poet extended the meaning of westwardness and eastwardness to the connotations the terms might assume with the earth regarded as a fixed center and the sun and stars conceived as revolving about it from east to west.

The poem, written in friendship for the Irish poet, Thomas McGreevy, is one of two under the general title, "Our Stars Come from Ireland." In the poem, the poet faces toward Ireland and sees the stars moving toward him—"an east in their compelling westwardness"—and thus the whole habit of his mind is changed from looking westward to looking eastward. Stevens wrote Thomas McGreevy that the poem did little more than make a point of "the westwardness of things." Yet the poem holds a connotation for westwardness as related to the passing away of things, and in the same sense eastwardness suggests the oncoming of things and events.[1] An image of morning at the end of the poem represents a change in the whole westward habit of mind because daybreak is a natural symbol of a beginning. The poem presents the onset of morning from over the ocean to the East, and in this eastwardness he finds at last the source of all westwardness:

> There was an end at which in a final change,
> When the whole habit of the mind was changed,
> The ocean breathed out morning in one breath.　　　(*CP*, 455)

Whatever importance Stevens ascribed to the impetus he received from an integration, he never forgot that its function was primarily inceptive. The letters to Latimer explained that ideas were only elements of a poem, that any subject was ancillary to the true purpose of all his beginnings; this purpose was simply the writing of poetry. Yet the specific concept, he surmised, opened the deep well of invention: "But sometimes it becomes a little more definite and fluid, and then the thing goes ahead rapidly" (*L*, 297).

III

"A poetic metaphor—that is to say, a metaphor poetic in a

1. A similar idea was expressed a number of years earlier in "The Well Dressed Man with a Beard." In this poem, "yes" is the equivalent of eastwardness and "no" of westwardness; things passing away are said to be disappearing with the setting sun—sliding "over the western cataract" (*CP*, 247).

sense more specific than the sense in which poetry and metaphor
are one—appears to be poetry at its source. It is, Stevens asserted
and then qualified his affirmation. "At least it is poetry at one of
its sources although not necessarily the most fecundating" (*NA*,
81). Because they are already conceived and separate for contemplation, metaphors, images, random lines or phrases incite
reaction, influence contingent meaning. Like any mark made by
the mind on the blank of the yet uncreated, a metaphor will en-
tail a flow of import, for what is made is evocative of what can be
made of it. In itself, a metaphor would tend to induce meaning
that is an extension of the literal or symbolic significance of the
two things compared. And as it works upon the poet's mind, it
will probably bring forth something latent and customary, some
import that the poet usually ponders when writing poetry, especially if the two images of which it is composed are recurrent and
native to his thought.

In one of his explicatory letters to Hi Simons, Stevens mentioned a metaphor that seemed to have elicited the ideas implied
in a poem of "Notes toward a Supreme Fiction" (*L*, 444–45).
"The blue woman was probably the weather of a Sunday morning early last April when I wrote this."[2] The metaphor remembered so casually in his letter had become in the poem a comparison of the blue sky to a woman looking from a window at the
phenomena of earth. As the image extended itself into meaning,
the idea of a personified sky probably led him to consider that

---

2. On another occasion, Stevens said that the weather around him was
written into a poem. "The weather as described is the weather that was
about me when I wrote this" (*L*, 434). The description is that of "Not to be
realized" in "Notes toward a Supreme Fiction" and is beautifully explicit:
"Weather by Franz Hals," and then in the next stanza, "Brushed up by
brushy winds in brushy clouds/Wetted by blue, colder for white" (*CP*, 385).
This poem of weather is discussed in detail in my book, *Stevens' Poetry of
Thought* (Baltimore: Johns Hopkins Press, 1966), pp. 111–14.

the blue woman looked upon truly objective reality, saw things as they were, for the blue day could have had no desire for the transformations of the human imagination:

> The blue woman, linked and lacquered, at her window
> Did not desire that feathery argentines
> Should be cold silver, neither that frothy clouds
>
> Should foam, be foamy waves, should move like them,
> Nor that the sexual blossoms should repose
> Without their fierce addictions.   (*CP*, 399)

The poem characterizes the blue woman as one who wishes to look at the external world directly, rather than by means of the subjective and interpretive vision of mind. "It was enough / For her that she remembered." What Stevens was considering when he wrote this line, so appropriately repeated, was left in doubt until he wrote the letter to Simons. Memory that could be attributed to the blue woman or the blue sky, had to be "the past, the routine, the mechanism" as Stevens tersely explained. This routine, this mechanism, was the repetition of the seasons, with seasonal things taking their place just as they always did—"free from change, and in its place everything had been right." In view of the fact that he said this was "a poem composed of the weather," its central figure must have been one of his many representations of nature as woman (*L*, 444–45).

It was in this vein that Stevens opened his explanation of the poem, for he seemed at first to be trying to make a distinction between a thing existing in itself and apart from the mind and the same thing existing as an image in consciousness. However, the distinction is specious. "The more exquisite the thing seen," he said, "the more exquisite the thing unseen" (*L*, 444). "The thing seen" is the thing as it is in the blue day, while "the thing unseen" is the image made within the self by perception. Yet "the thing seen" is *seen*; it too is perceived and must be an image in a mind.

Stevens' letter, and the poem as well, suggest a further possibility for the idea of the blue woman. The weather, the letter said, included not only "the time of year" but also "one's thoughts and feelings." And Stevens wrote of the opening of the poem as though the blue woman expressed his own feelings. "I had the feeling that the 'feathery argentines' were right and that it would not help to change them to something else, any more than it would help to metamorphize this, that or the other . . ." (*L*, 444–45).

Because of his use of the first person, it would seem that, in the image of the blue woman, Stevens was alluding to his desire for a poetry of plain reality, a desire he often mentioned in letters during the next decade. Thus, the suggestion arises that the blue woman represents the poet within him, fascinated by the reality of the world. The concluding sentence of his discussion of the poem enhances this implication: "Obviously in a poem composed of the weather and of things drifting round in it: the time of year and one's thoughts and feelings, the cold delineations round one take their places without help" (*L*, 445). His own words here, "the cold delineations *round one*" (the italics are mine), reveal that the blue woman is looking from the window of perception and has become for him mind as well as nature.[3] The conclusion of the poem illustrates beautifully the ambiguity of the woman figure:

The blue woman looked and from her window named

The corals of the dogwood, cold and clear,

3. This kind of double significance for an image occurs elsewhere in Stevens' work. The sun, for instance, is an image that holds a dual possibility and can be understood as a symbol of both the consciousness of reality and the idea of an objective reality.

Cold, coldly delineating, being real,
Clear and, except for the eye, without intrusion.

(*CP*, 399–400)

To name, to identify, to see things as they must be in themselves, is an act of pure intuition. And yet the dogwood blossoms are seen as corals and thus are interpreted metaphorically by the mind, as well as perceived.[4] Though the blue day holds the essential reality of the phenomena of its season, the human figure, the woman, is still dominant in the metaphor. These two elements, mind and nature, exert their alternating pull in the poem. Perhaps the alternation existed for the poet as he conceived the poem. Certainly it existed for him several years later when, in a letter, he spoke of "our occasional Northern mornings, the bluest in the world" and a few sentences later said that "it is not always easy to tell the difference here between thinking and looking out of the window" (*L*, 664).

IV

In "The Irrational Element in Poetry," Stevens disavowed any notion that there might be a certain way for a poem to be made. The choice of what he called "the subject matter" was completely irrational, he said. It was either "fortuitous" or its origin was "imperceptible." As for the development of a poem, he asserted that it was just as unpredictable as the choice of an idea for a poem (*OP*, 220–21). Thus the account in "A Collect of Philosophy" was not a description of a method but a recounting of elements in a

4. Helen Vendler also considers that the poem presents an idea of reality seen plainly and, at the same time, interpretively. Her analysis of this poem explains clearly the metaphors that occur in the poem's denials of the humanizing of phenomena by the blue woman. See Vendler, *On Extended Wings* (Cambridge: Harvard University Press, 1969), pp. 183–84.

contingent and unpredictable act. Each poem must have emerged
from a process that was the poem growing in its intrinsic way. And
what he said about the making of poems suggests that his constructive preparation may have been no more than a concentration
of long amorphous thinking, shaped by good fortune and good
habits of language and imagery, as well as by taste and reflection.
"The acquisitions of poetry are fortuitous; *trouvailles*," he said in
the "Adagia" (*OP,* 169).

Evidently it was a *trouvaille* that was the origin of "Bethou me,
said sparrow, to the crackled blade" in "Notes toward a Supreme
Fiction." The *trouvaille* was his phonetic rendering of the cry of a
catbird into the phrase, "bethou." His comments on this poem included memories of its inception and development. Among these
memories were certain details of his garden that contributed to the
making of the poem: the coppice, which he said was a small stand
of evergreens; crisp grass, leaves, and summer rain; wren, jay,
robin, and catbird; and the sparrow, which in the poem became a
paradigm of subjective will.

The integration that set in motion his thought about the poem
came to him from impressions of bird song in his garden. "This is
rather an old-fashioned poem of the onomatopoeia of a summer
afternoon," he said, recalling the circumstances of the genesis of
the poem (*L,* 435). The sound suggesting sense was the cry of a
catbird that resembled "bethou." The repetitious character of
bird sounds, he thought, had the effect of effacing individuality of
voice, just as the repetitions implicit in any generalization or
grouping such as species, class, or kind tended to obliterate the
individuality of the creature. "There is a repetition of a sound,
ké-ké, all over the place. Its monotony unites the separate sounds
into one, as a number of faces become one, as all fates become a
common fate, as all the bottles blown by a glass blower become
one, and as all bishops grow to look alike, etc." (*L,* 438).

The catbird's "bethou" among the trees in his garden, Stevens

remembered, interrrupted the monotony of the sound of "ké-ké."
Then he added, as though in explanation, "Of course, there may
be a psychological reason for the development of the idea" (*L*,
438). The "psychological reason" was the play of mind that heard
in the cry of a catbird an English phrase, "bethou." Doubtless the
phrase brought to mind "Ode to the West Wind" and Shelley's
wish that external force impart its vigor and creative powers to
his inner self: "Be thou me, impetuous one." When Stevens formed
his own idea from "bethou," he adapted it to one of his recurring
themes. The one appropriate to the phrase "bethou me" was the
idea that it is the nature of the self to make reality its own by
conceiving it in its individual way.

Stevens recalled his pleasure at the change of sound when the
catbird with its "bethou" (the cry was given to the sparrow in
the poem) seemed to mock the other birds; he recalled also how
the bird appeared to be the natural egotist invoking regard for its
subjectivity. "When the sparrow begins calling be-thou: *Bethou
me* (I have already said that it probably was a catbird) he expresses
one's own liking for the change; he invites attention from the
summer grass; he mocks the wren, the jay, the robin" (*L*, 438).
In the poem, the wren is bloody, the jay a felon, not only because
of the natural aggressiveness of these birds but also because they
are a part of the external world and external reality seems to the
individual self to be an opposing force—like the violence within
against the violence without of another context (*NA*, 36). Reality
that seems to oppose the self can be converted by the self into its
inner experience. Of the sparrow and its will to conceive reality,
as expressed by "bethou me," Stevens noted that "perhaps it
makes an image out of the force with which it struggles to survive." The self offers as a seduction to the opposing outer reality
this invitation to be transmuted into the imagery of its mind.
"Bethou is the spirit's own seduction," Stevens said (*L*, 438).

The germinating seed of the poem—"the onomatopoeia of a

summer afternoon"—must have been conceived as some version
of the basic idea of the whole composition at an early phase of the
meditation that shaped the poem. This basic idea is a simple
truism: the fact that only the individual creature has subjectivity,
that the type or universal is a lifeless abstraction repeated in each
of the individuals of the grouping. The basic idea probably divided
itself into two parts and gave the poem's flow of discourse a son-
netlike form. One of these two parts of the idea is expressed by
the opening stanzas, which celebrate the will of the living creature
to internalize and thus make the environing world its own:

> Bethou me, said sparrow, to the crackled blade,
> And you, and you, bethou me as you blow,
> When in my coppice you behold me be.
>
> Ah, ké! the bloody wren, the felon jay,
> Ké-ké, the jug-throated robin pouring out,
> Bethou, bethou, bethou me in my glade.   (*CP*, 393–94)

In comparison with the brute sound of "ké-ké" and the many
meaningless sounds made by physical accident, the voice of subjectivity seems to be heavenly music:

> There was such idiot minstrelsy in rain,
> So many clappers going without bells,
> That these bethous compose a heavenly gong.   (*CP*, 394)

The other idea Stevens developed from the initial integration—
that repetition absorbed individuality into the generic, the faceless
mass of things—was one suggested to him by the constant repetition of "ké-ké." The poem indicates that only the individual is
capable of subjective life, that when individuality is lost in generalization and becomes a generic figure—its own topological effigy—
then it is incapable of individual experience or imagination and is
thus "eye without lid, mind without any dream":

> One voice repeating, one tireless chorister,
> The phrases of a single phrase, ké-ké,
> A single text, granite monotony,
>
> One sole face, like a photograph of fate,
> Glass-blower's destiny, bloodless episcopus,
> Eye without lid, mind without any dream—
>
> These are of minstrels lacking minstrelsy,
> Of an earth in which the first leaf is the tale
> Of leaves, in which the sparrow is a bird
>
> Of stone, that never changes.   (CP, 394)

In the last two stanzas, the idea of subjectivity itself is regarded as one of the universal repetitions. The sparrow symbolizes the self, and now all sparrows are one. The repertory of individual song is absorbed into the total noise. "Bethou" is only another recurring sound:

> . . . Bethou him, you
> And you, bethou him and bethou. It is
> A sound like any other. It will end.   (CP, 394)

"In the face of death life asserts itself," Stevens said, as though in paraphrase and probably in reference to the poem's conclusion (L, 438). But he must have been drawn again into the train of thought that formed a background for the poem. For in the last lines, the poet speaks, not the sparrow, and "bethou him and bethou" is an adjuration to the other birds, the grass, the environing world to become the content of experience for the sparrow, as well as to exist apart. Then, assuming the cosmic view, he observes that the will of the conceiving self will cease like any other sound or will.

V

Another occasion on which Stevens revealed the beginning of a poem was in a letter answering questions asked by Hi Simons. "Anecdote of Canna," he said, "is the sort of poem that forms itself in one's mind" (*L*, 464). It formed while he was "killing time" at the capitol in Washington. The terraces there seemed to him so unreal that the effect "was more or less somnambulistic." The end of this almost-sleepwalking mood occurred when the notion that was the incipient idea of the poem came to him, the notion that "one never really thinks or thinks clearly in dreams." Two days later, he realized that he had related a memory and had not yet explained the poem. He then wrote a note to Simons paraphrasing the poem (*L*, 465).

Apparently, this creative experience—that of a poem forming in his mind—was typical for him. Although he made notes, sometimes tentative versions of longer projects, he composed more in meditation than on paper. He pondered the thought of a poem before the poetry itself came to him—as another poem expresses it, before "the vital music formulates the words" (*CP*, 259). "Besides, I am at work on something else at the moment," he said of some poem that was developing in his mind, "and, while I am not particularly active about it, still it is going on all the time . . ." (*L*, 354). And when a poem began to coalesce into language, he might hold it all in his mind before committing it to paper. "Sometimes when I am writing a thing, it is complete in my own mind," he said of this ability to compose in meditation (*L*, 403). But again, he might find it necessary to note, on whatever scraps of paper were at hand, the beginning of what came to him on his walks, so that he could keep it from vanishing while thinking of what was to follow. "I have to jot things down as I go along since, otherwise, by the time I got to the end of the poem I should have forgotten the beginning" (*L*, 844). Although he did work later on the typescript, essentially a poem was composed before it was written. This is why Stevens could say that he had no manuscripts in the usual sense of the word.[5]

"It takes a great deal of thought to come to the points that concern me—and I am, at best, an erratic and inconsequential thinker" (*L*, 186). Stevens spoke in this way of his preparation of the discourse of a poem the year he wrote "Sunday Morning." And many years later, he still referred to the kind of erratic thought that was productive of poetry with the phrase "the vagaries of poetic thinking." This letter from 1942 is especially interesting because, by carefully reading its implications, some of the meditative background of a poem can be divined (*L*, 402–4). "On an Old Horn" was conceived entirely in his mind, Stevens said, and written just as it was, fresh from the creative thought. In apology for its possible obscurity, he said that "I write it in my own way and don't care what happens."

When examined in close comparison with the poem, his discussion seems to be more of a recollection of the meditation from which the poem emerged than an explication of the poem itself. Stevens realized this toward the end of his 1942 letter. "This is not just an explanation; I remember very well that this is the sort of thing that produced the poem" (*L*, 404).

Stevens apparently had been thinking about the unity of all organic life. "Man sees reflections of himself in nature," he remarked, to give the background of thought that preceded the poem. Extending his thought further, he explained that one could begin again at another point in the chain of life and suppose that birds might see reflections of themselves in men instead of the

5. Although Stevens suggested that he did little more than "pull and tug at the typed script" of a poem, there may have been more revision than this phrase indicated (*L*, 844). The revision of "From the Journal of Crispin" that resulted in "The Comedian as the Letter C" revealed the amount of emendation he was willing to undertake to satisfy himself. See Louis Martz's essay on this revision (*WS*, 3–29).

other way around. "Suppose we start all over again; we start as birds, say, and see reflections of ourselves in man: perhaps we were men once, or we may even become men" (*L*, 403). Here we have the train of thought from which the poem issued and, thus entering into the poem through the poet's prior meditation, we can continue with the poem's first stanza and its birds that once were men:

> The bird kept saying that birds had once been men,
> Or were to be, animals with men's eyes,
> Men fat as feathers, misers counting breaths,
> Women of a melancholy one could sing.   (*CP*, 230)

Stevens' explanation of his train of thought reveals that the poem is a meditation concerned with the kind of naturalism implicit in much of his poetry and plainly stated at a later date to another correspondent: "One of my firm beliefs is that Life and Nature are one" (*L*, 533).

Stevens' account of the meditation that produced the poem offered one version of this thesis, the idea that the many voices of life and the voice of nature are one. "It follows that a lion roaring in a desert and a boy whistling in the dark are alike, playing old horns: an old horn, perhaps the oldest horn" (*L*, 404). Thus all utterances, the voices of birds and the voices of men, make up the one sound that is the oldest: the expressive being of nature.

In his meditation, he conceived the horn as more than animal noise. The horn that each one toots is also each creature's individual conception of things. It is all one has, according to the poet. Pursuing his thought further, he said that "one has, after all, only one's own horn on which to toot, one's own synthesis on which to rely" (*L*, 403). The bird, tooting on his horn, finds in his own expression of his individuality the strength of a man or, even more, strength to face finality. The poem's version of the idea indicated

that the man was created in the voice that was his voice and yet
also the voice of nature:

> In the little of his voice, or the like,
> Or less, he found a man, or more, against
> Calamity, proclaimed himself, was proclaimed.   (*CP*, 230)

Stevens' letter omitted part of the environing meditation of the
poem. He did not recall, apparently, the thought surrounding the
lines that preceded those quoted above. It would seem from these
lines that Stevens was engaged in a reflection about the universal question regarding all individual conception. The question, as
implied in the poem, was whether experience of an environing
world—be it that of men or birds—is an imagining of something
that cannot be realized as it is, or whether experience is an exact
reflection of an outer reality:

> . . . The bird then boomed.
> Could one say that he sang the colors in the stones,
> False as the mind, instead of the fragrance, warm
> With sun?   (*CP*, 230)

Part II of "On an Old Horn" was apparently another voice
with another thought, almost a fragment of another poem. The
disparity was caused by the omission of any hint in the poem of
the continuance of the train of thought that produced the whole
poem, except for the tooting of the horn phonetically, in "pipperoo,
pippera, pipperum":

> If the stars that move together as one, disband,
> Flying like insects of fire in a cavern of night,
> Pipperoo, pippera, pipperum . . . The rest is rot.   (*CP*, 230)

Stevens' letter filled in the apparent break in continuity of
thought: "one's own fortitude of spirit is the only 'fester Burg';
without that fortitude one lives in chaos" (*L*, 403). This sentence

indicated that the meditative setting of part II was an extension of the idea from part I that each had only his own synthesis of things with which to meet the chaos of infinite possibility; each self, out of his own fortitude of spirit, must formulate and conceive his own individual sense of the world. In the next sentence of the letter, recalling the environment of thought from which part II arose, he implied that the ability to conceive order in the mind of each of us enables us to create order rather than chaos; however, the opposite was also possible. "Suppose, now, we try the thing out, let the imagination create chaos by conceiving of it." This is prefatory thinking. With this background of thought given, he paraphrased the stanza: "The stars leave their places and move about aimlessly, like insects on a summer night. Now, a final toot on the horn.[6] That is all that matters. The order of the spirit is the only music of the spheres: or, rather, the only music" (*L*, 403).

In Stevens' naturalism, man is always a part of nature. "The order of the spirit" is simply the order that is an individual mind. The thought and symbolism in this poem are as typical of Stevens as the method of writing off the top of a prior meditation. For instance, "One's own synthesis on which to rely" (*L*, 403) is the mind's integration of reality, the world as it seems in each consciousness at each instant.

Steven's analysis of "On an Old Horn" is discussed at some length because it describes part of a train of thought that entered into the making of a poem. After the import was absorbed in the imagery and incident that embodied it, Stevens' genius for language enabled him to create a wording fitted to the nature of

---

6. This phrase of Stevens, "Now a final toot on the horn" and the title, "On an Old Horn," probably reflect an old folk saying. In Scott's *The Fortunes of Nigel,* King James says that a Puritan is only one of the same kind as a "Papist." Puritanism, he says, is "a tout on an auld horn."

the poetic concept that emerged from the prior meditation. The result is original, striking, tacit, sometimes almost aphoristic, and nearly always a complete unit—even when part of a series or group of poems. The preliminary thinking would vanish and idea would become absorbed into poetry because the poet subordinated the element of thought to the poem's achievement as a composition.

Three

A POSSIBLE FOR ITS POSSIBLENESS

I

Because so much of Stevens' poetry is a cluster of intimation, one person's understanding of one of his poems may seem a misunderstanding to another. Intimation points toward abstraction, and thus what is often in question is the amount and character of idea in a poem. As a rule, Stevens' ideas are indeterminate because they are usually only half developed, as well as only half revealed. The tacit part is hidden in the spaces of ellipses, or it hovers over scenes and figures. In one of the "Adagia," Stevens indicates his awareness of latent abstraction in his own poetry by a statement about poetry in general: "Every poem is a poem within a poem: the poem of the idea within the poem of the words" (OP, 174). He said once that "words are thoughts" (NA, 32) and thus must have meant by "the poem of the idea" a meaning implicit within the overt statement of "the poem of the words." In praise of "the poem of the idea," he wrote that "the thing said must be the poem not the language used in saying it. At its best the poem consists of both elements" (*OP*, 165). In contradiction, he maintained that "when we find in poetry that which gives us a momentary existence on an exquisite plane, is it necessary to ask the meaning of the poem?" (*OP*, 223).

When Stevens wrote on the language of poetry in "The Noble Rider and the Sound of Words," he disclosed the affection and care with which he achieved the "unalterable vibration," the finality of phrasing of his great style, both early and late. Poetry's language, he said, fills a human need for sound as well as meaning and "makes us listen to words when we hear them, loving them and feeling them, makes us search the sound of them, for a finality, a perfection, an unalterable vibration, which it is only within the power of the acutest poet to give them." And then he added: "Above everything else, poetry is words," and again, for emphasis, "words, above everything else, are, in poetry, sounds." But just before this he had said that poetry was language and language a possibility of thought: "Words are thoughts and not only our own thoughts but the thoughts of men and women ignorant of what it is that they are thinking" (*NA*, 32). These quotations reflect a poet in love with words as a given—as what they are in their immediacy of sound and sense—as well as fascinated with the possibility of words, with what they may create in the silence beyond the voice.

The given of a poem is its discourse, its sound and statement. The possible within that discourse is a wordless and indeterminate meaning open to conjecture. Although the possible is dependent on the given, any specific conjecture about it is separated from the poem and is only the making of the reader. Possibility is intrinsic to the nature of a Stevens poem and, after each conjecture, the possible is still unresolved and open for another conjecture. Certainly Stevens never thought that in an implication there was one certain meaning hidden in the act of creating it—the poem's sealed letter to the reader, to be opened only by the poet or some ideal intuitive critic. "The poem is the poem," he says, "not its paraphrase" (*L,* 362). When he wrote explanations of some poems, Stevens knew that then he was not the maker giving his poems exact meaning; he had become a reader offering conjectures. Something of this kind must have been in his mind when he said of his paraphrase of one poem: "It makes one say a good many things that are true only when they are not said this way" (*L,* 360).

In Stevens' poetry, the possible is often a field of implication radiating from a center of concept that is either stated or itself implied. Possibility lies in unspoken connectives between disjunctive passages; accumulated symbolic import; and the simple connotations carried by scenes, situations, figures, images of many kinds. Of course, in an ultimate sense, there is no true denotation. By the very nature of language, meaning is always evoked and thus only possible. Yet meaning is more or less signified, given in some way.

Allowing for a practical distinction between given and possible meaning, the question arises of how much of the possible was formulated in the poet's mind when conceiving the poem. Perhaps the language actually given in the poem was what became explicit for the poet, and the wordless hovering elements never emerged from the unconscious base of creative thought. Or it may be that the latent meanings (at least some of them) were entertained in meditation, although still indefinite, and that it was determined then that they should be possible rather than given. In most cases, it is at least a reasonable conjecture to suppose that the poem was conceived on the levels that subsist in print, allowing for much emendation, or even for little, as seems often to be true of Stevens. Some of the possible is beyond the reach of language and can only be suggested. Some of the given must have been realized as it is because of a love of language as sound, with meaning emerging in its wake.

Sometimes, however, the possible must have been known and deliberately left unsaid. The second poem of "Le Monocle de Mon Oncle" was probably deepened intentionally by signifying through implication what might have been too simple, too plain for enunciation. The poem consists of four passages with only slight overt connections. The first is a scene, the second a metaphor resembling a riddle, the third an avowal of a personal situation, the fourth an admonition. The opening line, with its red bird and golden floor, is a verbal illustration reminiscent of the miniatures in red and gold within initial letters of illuminated texts. The first four lines present, as though the poet preferred a picture to a statement, one of the most conventional, most repeated themes for poems—the ardors of spring and love and song:

> A red bird flies across the golden floor.
> It is a red bird that seeks out his choir
> Among the choirs of wind and wet and wing.
> A torrent will fall from him when he finds. (*CP*, 13)

In the second passage, he asks about the poetry of love and springtime: "Shall I uncrumple this much-crumpled thing?" With this question he describes by metonymy the kind of poetry that has been used too many times—written, he implies, on the crumpled paper of many other poets. The latent answer to the interrogative becomes the connection to the third passage. Yes, the poet answers by implication, with the difference that years and experience make, for many springs and much love and song give me in my declining years the sense of one leaving behind what the young enter upon:

> I am a man of fortune greeting heirs;
> For it has come that thus I greet the spring.

These choirs of welcome choir for me farwell.
No spring can follow past meridian.   (*CP*, 13)

In the concluding lines, the poet then addresses the companion, the beloved of all the other poems of "Le Monocle de Mon Oncle." The break from the preceding lines is very slight:

Yet you persist with anecdotal bliss
To make believe a starry *connaissance*.   (*CP*, 13)

Paraphrase shows that the given meaning carries only a part of the total import. Although I am past the time, the poet indicates, when I can enjoy the quality of life and love suggested by youth and spring, nevertheless you continue to recall our springtime ardors and in this way try to retain our youthful idealized relationship or "starry *connaissance*"—"starry" with the connotation it has in the trite phrase, "starry-eyed," and "*connaissance*" in the sense of a knowing, a familiarity of one with another.

Quite possibly, the use of implication and ellipse in this poem was contrived, its discourse deliberately truncated, just as the pronoun was deleted after the word "finds" in the line, "A torrent will fall from him when he finds." Stevens' letters are of no help here.

In the case of another poem, XXXVIII of "Like Decorations in a Nigger Cemetery," he left no doubt but that he intentionally made its central theme no more than possible. Stevens explained to Hi Simons that the real subject was tacit; in spite of what was expressed in the poem's wording, "the poem of the idea" was not concerned with what that wording expressed. Thus when he conceived the wording of the poem, he must have thought of withholding its central concern and intended its discourse to be innuendo.

Evidently this is one of those poems in which Stevens feels the dominance of reality over the imagination. "Do not show me Corot while it is still summer," he says in paraphrase of the given meaning. "Do not show me pictures of summer while it is still summer; even the mist is golden; wait until a little later" (*L*, 349). The poem is composed of three seemingly discrete statements.[1] The first, as he says, refers to Corot as the painter of autumn landscapes, whose album is paradigm for any work of art. The sky of the second line must be the darker sky of winter. The mist of the third line is not "wholly mist" because its gold is sunlight. Any conjecture of a pun in "wholly mist" must be rejected as inappropriate to the context as paraphrased by Stevens:

> The album of Corot is premature.
> A little later when the sky is black.
> Mist that is golden is not wholly mist. (*CP*, 156)

Since Stevens says of these lines that "while expressed in terms of autumn [they] do not concern autumn," one might expect his explanation to tell what they do concern. Instead, he gives the paraphrase of the discourse as quoted above and deliberately leaves the poem's "concern" an undefined possibility. Interpretation can conjecture that this concern might be described thus, using the manner of paraphrase: no work of the imagination can rival the reality before the observer. There is also this other conjecture: art is constructed from experience, but tardily and with a difference. The second possibility must be preferred in view of the echo of this poem that occurs in his essay, "The Relations between Poetry and Painting": "The mind retains experience, so that long after the experience, ... long after the limpid vistas of Corot, that faculty within us of which I have spoken makes its own constructions out of that experience" (*NA*, 164).

This theory that art or poetry emerges from long past and

---

1. Helen Vendler, on p. 71 of *On Extended Wings* (Cambridge: Harvard University Press, 1969), fills out the spaces of ellipses in this poem. With her "missing links," the poem then reads as a complete given.

buried experience is one of the possible meanings to be inferred
from "Infernale," a poem sent to Ronald Lane Latimer in its
final form in 1935, but perhaps written earlier (*L*, 285–86).[2] It is
one of those Stevens poems in which the given meaning opens
almost like allegory onto a field of unspoken meaning yet ex-
ceeds allegory in its area of multiple possibility. The poem is a dialogue between "a boor of night" and "the living Proserpine."
"Night in middle earth"—the night within the body—would indicate the unconscious or subconscious, to use the term Stevens
favored. The boor with his fear of light or consciousness is a personification of the inertia that withholds elements of the unconscious from rising to conscious attention—elements like old, and
hence dead, experiences:

> (*A boor of night in middle earth cries out.*)
> Hola! Hola! What steps are those that break
> This crust of air? . . . (He pauses.) Can breath shake
> The solid wax from which the warmth dies out?
>
> I saw a waxen woman in a smock
> Fly from the black toward the purple air.
> (He shouts.) Hola! Of that strange light, beware!
>
> <div align="right">(<i>L</i>, 285–86)</div>

The passage in the poem, "Can breath shake/The solid wax from
which the warmth dies out," is a key to a figurative understanding
of the poem. "Solid wax" suggests the formed and unalterable
character of past experience, and "breath" has connotations for
utterance, for words:

---

2. "Infernale" was the title used in *Opus Posthumous* and hence is better
known than "The Guide of Alcestis," the title of the revised version of the
poem used here.

(Her pale smock sparkles in a light begun
To be diffused, and, as she disappears,
The silent watcher, far below her, hears:)
The soaring mountains glitter in the sun.   (L, 286)

If the poem's little drama is considered to be a sort of masque presenting the emergence of poetry from its unconscious ground, then Proserpine becomes an anima figure emerging from that "middle earth." She would personify an idea or "an integration" rising from its ground in past or dead experience to soar into consciousness as a poem, reaching Olympian heights, the peaks of conscious achievement.

The boor of "Infernale" is one of the many persons in Stevens' poetry that seems to embody some indefinite but presumable idea. Such others as Chieftain Iffucan, Belshazzar, Lady Howzen, Ercole, Jaffa, and Canon Aspirin continually invite conjecture by their air of implicit significance. By virtue of seeming to hold some special import, Stevens' exponible terms—for example, middle and Mediterranean; major man; the first idea; and certain otherwise ordinary words like summer and winter, skeleton, night, poverty, holiday, giant—all enhance the aura of possibility that surrounds these poems. With only a limited capacity for explicit meaning, these figures and terms suggest open perspectives of further reference.

It should not be assumed that this incertitude is devoid of semantic value. Certainly something should be resolved, choices made, probability set forth. The nature of possibility is continually to invite definition and eventually to escape it. However, when a seemingly indicative figure or term or cryptic usage of a word is explained by the poet himself, then the indefinite reference of that figure or term or word seems to emerge from the possible into the given. As a rule, the emergence is specious, for Stevens' explanations usually substitute one ambiguity for another.

II

Stevens' comments on his poems often paraphrased the given. Occasionally he also offered some formulation of the possible. In a note on "Gray Stones and Gray Pigeons," he insisted that the poem was its discourse. Then he conceded that there might be an implied meaning within its wording that he could interpret. "I suppose that there is an abstraction implicit in what is actually on the page, and that it would be something like this: everything depends on its sanction; and when its sanction is lost that is the end of it. But the poem is precisely what is printed on the page" (*L*, 347–48).[3]

But a poem was not altogether what was printed on the page, as Stevens indicated in "A Note on 'Les Plus Belles Pages,'" written for the Lamont Library at Harvard (*OP*, 293–94). He began his note with a comparison of what the poem seemed to say with what it seemed to imply. "Apparently the poem means," he began, but then he continued: "What it really means is . . ." What he stated as the meaning of the given was instead a conclusion that, by its nature, was a form of the possible. This conclusion was drawn from a conjunction of two separate parts of the poem. Of the two parts, the first was:

> The milkman came in the moonlight and the moonlight
> Was less than moonlight. Nothing exists by itself.
> The moonlight seemed to.   (*CP*, 244)

The other part was in the third stanza:

> The automaton, in logic self-contained,
> Existed by itself. Or did the saint survive?
> Did several spirits assume a single shape?   (*CP*, 245)

---

3. Stevens precedes this explanation by speaking of "destroying a poem by explaining it" (*L*, 347). However, few poets have ever been as generous as Stevens with explanation of their poems.

Stevens said about these two passages that the poem seemed to draw an equivalence between milkman and moonlight and logician and saint. Then he corrected this seeming by a far leap into the possible: "What it really means is that the inter-relation between things is what make them fecund" (*OP*, 293). In the poem, there was a list of things that illustrated, he said, his principle of the fecundity of interrelationship: "Two people, three horses, an ox / And the sun, the waves together in the sea" (*CP*, 245). He said that "interaction is the source of poetry" (*OP*, 293–94), and this was what he meant by his title, "Les Plus Belles Pages." The most beautiful pages were poetry, the consequence of the interrelation of intelligence and imagination. Then he departed from his poem to pursue the train of thought that his generalization had impelled. This was the sort of thing he often did in the course of explaining a poem and thus is worth quoting: "The inter-relation between reality and the imagination is the basis of the character of literature. The inter-relation between reality and the emotions is the basis of the vitality of literature, between reality and thought, the basis of its power" (*OP*, 294).

Stevens' one explication of a specific line in this poem was his statement that the last line, "Theology after breakfast sticks to the eye," was a rejection of any idea that the theology of Aquinas was involved in this poem. The line expressed its meaning by innuendo, and hence his explanation was again a formulation of the possible. He offered very little help for the rest of the poem. Apparently he thought that the reader would see the figure of the milkman as a paradigm of the ordinary self, the everyday consciousness, and the moonlight in its usual symbolic relationship with imagination.

He did not explain one contradiction in the poem's wording: "Nothing exists by itself" (*CP*, 244), and then later, "the automaton, in logic self-contained, / Existed by itself" (*CP*, 245). Stevens apparently became so interested in his idea of the fecundity of interrelationships that he forgot the third stanza, the source of the poem's problems. Perhaps "the automaton, in logic self-contained" was a reference to the *Summa Theologica*. And perhaps in the question about the saint, Stevens asked if his prodigious love of God, the essence of sainthood, survived the logician in him. The man, Aquinas, would contain both logician and saint and hence several selves or "spirits." Thus the question, "Did several spirits assume a single shape?" would induce an unspoken affirmative reply.

III

There are times when Stevens' explanations of poems are hard to reconcile with "what is printed on the page." Then it seems he must have written the comment on the poem without a clear recollection of its wording. He once apologized to Renato Poggioli for an explanation at variance with the wording of the poem. "My first explanation is nonsense, because it was made without considering the context. Just laziness on my part, for which I apologize" (*L,* 790).

His comments on "The Man with the Blue Guitar," XXIV are particularly interesting because they seem to confuse some of the wording of the poem with what is possible rather than what is given. The opening lines express his exalted feeling for the poetry he is creating or finding. "A poem like a missal found/In the mud" suggests that the language of a poem is almost hallowed and that it is found within the unstructured mass that is the primal state of language when it is no more than a potential in the unconscious. Stevens, who felt that one is composed of many selves, speaks in this poem as the creating self and refers to the realizing self as the scholar, the self that hungers for the perfected language of poetry, for a book, a page, even a phrase.[4] The poem that is a

4. In the "Adagia," he mentions the idea that one is composed of many selves. "The subjects of one's poems are the symbols of one's self or of one of one's selves" (*OP,* 164).

missal is come upon, is created, for that young man—the poet's intelligence—who realizes or reads the poem as it is created or found:

> That scholar hungriest for that book,
> The very book, or, less, a page
>
> Or, at the least, a phrase, that phrase,
> A hawk of life, that latined phrase.   (*CP*, 178)

The phrase is "latined" because it is learned, in that it contains a profundity. In his comment on the poem, Stevens transfers the word "latined" to the scholar when he refers to him as the one to whom "one addresses oneself for all his latined learning" (*L*, 360). The confusion is natural if one considers that Stevens is speaking as the one who creates the poem, as well as the one who realizes it and thus reads it. His explanations rarely reveal the identity of his personifications, and in this comment on the poem he mentions the secrecy that should prevail between the poet and his poem. However, he does say that the scholar is the one with "brooding-sight"—a way of looking or "a knowledge that seizes life, with joy in his eye":

> . . . a missal for brooding-sight.
> To meet that hawk's eye and to flinch
>
> Not at the eye but at the joy of it.
> I play. But this is what I think.   (*CP*, 178)

In one of his letters, Stevens also confuses this poem's language, its expressive phrasing, with the scholar who hungers to read or realize it. The joy that in the poem is such that one must "flinch" at it seems to be a light in the scholar's eye. But Stevens explains that the hawk's eye belongs to one of those phrases—"a hawk of life," he calls it—"that grips in its talons some aspect of life that it took a hawk's eye to see" (*L*, 783–84). The confusion arises again because the scholar is part of the one who is speaking, the poet, and is easily identified with what the creating self finds or makes.

In the last line of the poem, the creating self says, "I play." Stevens explains that "even though I recognize that I am satisfying the scholar to whom I am addressing myself, I pretend not to do so; I simply go on playing a tune" (*L,* 361). The creating self pretends that it does not address any idea, any meaning to the scholar, the receiving, listening, realizing consciousness. It pretends instead to go on playing the tune, the pure poem of sound. Nevertheless, the meaning his language implies is, he says, what he thinks. "Some aspect of life that it took a hawk's eye to see," Stevens says in order to depict the possible as a concept gripped by the talons of the phrase that is "a hawk of life" (*L,* 784). Thus "the poem of the idea" is held in implication and is not necessarily what is said, but in the poem's words "what I think." The secrecy that must prevail between the poet and his poem is the secrecy, as he says in his notes on the poem, of its never-resolved meaning, its possibility.

IV

What Stevens wished to avoid when writing his correspondents about his poems was any notion that there might be one certain possibility in a poem that, when formulated, would have the effect of the definiteness of the given. That he intended his poems to have a great deal of undefined potential is evident from a letter quoted in *The Explicator.* Stevens is speaking of works of the imagination—of poems, for instance: "It is not possible to attach a single, rational meaning to such things without destroying the imaginative or emotional ambiguity or uncertainty that is inherent in them and that is why poets do not like to explain. That the meanings given by others are sometimes meanings not intended by the poet or that were never present in his mind does not impair them as meanings.[5]

In spite of a dislike for explanations, he wrote friends and critics many comments on his poems. His explanations often paraphrased the discourse or reflected remnants of some meditation that prepared the poem. Occasionally, however, he does offer a glimpse of his sense of the possibility within a poem. Speaking of "The Man with the Blue Guitar," XXXII, he said, "This poem depends a good deal on its implications." Obviously, then, he intended the poem to hold more possible than given meaning. His paraphrase states that to be oneself in the poem, you should be "not as one really is but as one of the jocular procreations of the dark, of space" (*L*, 364):

> How should you walk in that space and know
> Nothing of the madness of space,
>
> Nothing of its jocular procreations?
> Throw the lights away. Nothing must stand
>
> Between you and the shapes you take
> When the crust of shape has been destroyed.
>
> You as your are? You are yourself.
> The blue guitar surprises you.   (*CP*, 183)

What implications of this poem are so important to Stevens?

---

5. Max Herzberg, "Stevens' 'The Emperor of Ice Cream,'" *The Explicator* 7, no. 5 (1948): 18. This quotation and others in the letters, especially a letter on p. 346, shows Stevens' awareness of scholarly discussion of "the intentional fallacy." This letter from 1940 precedes by six years the first appearance (in the *Sewanee Review*) of the most famous analysis of the problem of the author's intention. See W. K. Wimsatt and M. C. Beardsley, "The Intentional Fallacy," reprinted in W. K. Wimsatt, *The Verbal Icon* (Lexington: University of Kentucky Press, 1954), pp. 3–18.

Although he will not reveal them, he does hint at the unspoken central meaning. "The point of the poem is, not that this can be done," he says, referring to being oneself not as one is, "but as one of the jocular procreations of the dark, of space." Then he gives an inkling of the possible: "but that, if done, it is the key to poetry, to the closed garden, if I may become rhapsodic about it, of the fountain of youth and life and renewal" (*L*, 364).[6]

This must be a poem about creativity, as he suggests. Significance can be found for its imagery in Stevens' explanation of "Sombre Figuration," a poem of the same period as "The Man with the Blue Guitar." His comment on "Sombre Figuration" speaks of "the illimitable space of the sub-conscious" and says of the conscious and the subconscious that "they are the world in which we live and move" (*L*, 373–74). The opening line of the poem, "Throw away the lights, the definitions," indicates a turning from the conscious intelligence to the darkness of subconscious space. On these terms, then, "the dark, the space" is the creative unconscious, and to become one of its "jocular procreations" is to become open to the fountains of invention, to the spontaneities of free imaginative process. This, he says, is "the key to poetry." Speaking many years later of variants on one's identity, he says that "the self consists of endless images" (*L*, 670), and this notion seems to echo the idea suggested by "the shapes you take/When the crust of shape has been destroyed."

---

6. Harold Bloom observes that "this is major Stevens" and goes on to indicate the significance of Stevens' comment on the poem. He says, "the blue guitar surprises Stevens as it surprises us." He reveals the importance of the word *surprise,* showing that "Stevens' poem suddenly has seized its poet and its reader together." He explains "that to be 'surprised' means to be captured or to be taken hold of without warning." See Bloom, *Wallace Stevens: The Poems of Our Climate* (Ithaca, N.Y.: Cornell University Press, 1976), p. 134.

The "crust of shape" would be, it seems, the self of conventional presence.

From these remarks of Stevens' and the inferences to be drawn from them, we can conclude that the key to the closed garden of creativity is the subjectivity that is truly oneself as one might be in one's own unique poems. The blue guitar that surprises the poet, although usually the imagination in a larger sense, is here the instrument that plays to the poet his poetry. In this regard he can say to himself: "You are yourself." It is like an echo of the conclusion of an earlier poem: "And there I found myself more truly and more strange" (*CP*, 65).

V

Many of Stevens' poems seem to have been conceived as a literal text with an indefinite figurative, metaphorical, or symbolic potential. This is a useful way of considering the given and the possible when the given is a scene or situation evocative of one of Stevens' recurring ideas. From the tenor of Stevens' many explanations of poems, the possible does not lend itself to point-by-point correlation with the given, and figurative possibility in his poetry always falls short of the allegorical. Sometimes it is no more than the expansion of an image or scene or situation from a particular to a universal, as in synechdoche. For instance, "Earthy Anecdote," by its characterization and action, appears to hold symbolic meaning, but Stevens himself cancels this possibility. "There's no symbolism in the 'Earthy Anecdote.' There's a good deal of theory about it, however; but explanations spoil things" (*L*, 204). And later he said, "I intended something quite concrete: actual animals . . ." (*L*, 209). Whatever theory there is must be an idea about the poem and not an idea to be found in it.

The movement of the poem is faintly reminiscent of an amusing verse Stevens wrote as a boy in a letter to his mother at a

time when the moon was full, and as he said, so was everyone
else:

> Oh! hic—keep to the middle of the road
> Oh!　"　　"　"　"　　"　"　　"
> Don't look to the right
> Don't look to the left
> But keep to the middle of the road.　　　　　　(*L,* 7)

In "Earthy Anecdote," the poet is a choreographer and the earthy creatures of his poem are universal figures whose life activity
is formalized as though in dance:

> The bucks clattered.
> The firecat went leaping,
> To the right, to the left,
> And
> Bristled in the way.
>
> Later, the firecat closed his bright eyes
> And slept.　　　　　　　　　　　　　　　(*CP,* 3)

In view of Stevens' remark about it, the poem must remain close
to the literal. On this level, it becomes a stylization of evasion
and pursuit, of the animal relationship of hunter and hunted and
an anecdote of hunger and satiety.

VI

Many of Stevens' poems stand in all the perfection of their
language on the literal level, without any need for metaphorical
extension; yet, a figurative possibility may hover beyond, unrealized and therefore undefined. This is especially true of several
poems of his later period. Stevens' letters offer little guidance for
exploration of the possible in these poems, for there is a paucity

of explanations of poems after "Notes toward a Supreme Fiction." Although the possible in the later poetry cannot be extrapolated in terms of any comment referring to a specific passage, some remark or comment in another context may be illuminating When an image or other element of the given can be associated with some use or identification of that image by Stevens, then there is a tendency in the given to suggest that use or identification as a possible meaning for the image. Recurrence of elements— image, idea, phrase—from poem to poem offers one kind of identification; a mention of some habitually used analogy may offer another.

When he was at work on his last book, Stevens told Barbara Church that he habitually felt an analogy between creative work and reading. "Often when I am writing poetry I have in mind an image of reading a page of a large book: I mean the large page of a book. What I read is what I like" (*L,* 642).[7] Any Stevens poem dominated by the image of someone reading a book, even if it was written somewhat before the date of this letter (1949), must hold in possibility the idea that the poem in some way is concerned with the writing or making of poetry. Of course, something in the context of a poem may cancel that influence. For example, in "Phosphor Reading by His Own Light," the line that speaks of the reader as a realist would seem to exempt this poem from the sway of Stevens' mention of his usual connection of the act of writing with the image of reading. For the book in this poem, like that in the much earlier poem, "The Reader," seems to be the book of unfolding experience.

"The House Was Quiet and the World Was Calm" holds no element to cancel the influence of the poet's association of writing poetry and reading a book. Usually the poem is seen in isolation

---

7. For a brief analysis of this association of writing and reading, see in this book the conclusion of the first section of Chapter 1.

and therefore on the literal, rather than the figurative, level. Because of this association of writing and reading for the creating poet, the account in this poem of an experience of deep concentration on a book may assume the character of an account of deep concentration while writing a poem. Then the calmness of the world becomes the condition of creative meditation and the quiet of the house an effect of the poet's absorption in his work. In the same way, the reader becomes the book because the poem he is writing completely fills his mind. Then the summer night of that experience is one with the life of language and thought of the poem growing at that moment. Stevens often identified night with the creative unconscious and summer with immediate experience.[8] "The words were spoken as if there was no book" can be understood as an allusion to the words, the lines that come to the poet as he conceives his poem. He has not written them down, but he hears them as though spoken. And they are spoken by the mind to which they occur:

> The house was quiet and the world was calm.
> The reader became the book; and summer night
>
> Was like the conscious being of the book.
> The house was quiet and the world was calm.
>
> The words were spoken as if there was no book,
> Except that the reader leaned above the page,
>
> Wanted to lean, wanted much most to be
> The scholar to whom his book is true, to whom

8. For the connotations night holds for Stevens, there are these passages: "Night and the imagination being one" (*OP,* 71) and "Night is the nature of man's interior world" (*CP,* 333). For the connotations summer holds for Stevens, there is this explanation: "reality was the summer of the title of the book . . ." (*L,* 719). The book is his own *Transport to Summer.* Immediate experience of the world is implied here by the word "reality."

The summer night is like a perfection of thought.
The house was quiet because it had to be.

The quiet was part of the meaning, part of the mind:
The access of perfection to the page.   (*CP*, 358)

In the "Adagia," Stevens says that "poetry is the scholar's art" (*OP*, 167). As part of the possibility suggested for this poem, the scholar would be the creating poet rather than the scholarly reader, and the quiet as the poet's concentration would be part of his meaning and would bring the poem he writes its "access of perfection." In one of his letters about the writing of poems, Stevens says that a poem's language has its own unique idiom. "The access of perfection" in the poem quoted above would be its own expressive wording. The poem's expressive language, Stevens says in his letter, "seems to be one of the consequences of concentration. I should like to undertake the job of establishing the place of concentration in this sort of thing" (*L*, 500).

In "The House Was Quiet and the World Was Calm," the given is a description of a state of deep concentration. The possible issues from the given, and in this way the oneness of the scholar and his book (or the seeming oneness of the summer with the book), are an effect of concentration. "The truth in a calm world" is what is said in the poem that the poet is making. In the closed world of his concentration, there can be no other meaning for him:

. . . The truth in a calm world,
In which there is no other meaning, itself

Is calm, itself is summer and night, itself
Is the reader leaning late and reading there.   (*CP*, 359)

A literal understanding of the poem is usually the preferred reading. This kind of understanding has been aptly described by Joseph Riddel "as the perfect communion of self and other," a condition he finds set forth in a passage from Santayana: ". . . as in reading a book, the material book is forgotten, and the reader lives in rehearsing the author's thoughts without thinking of the author."[9] The quotation is very close to the given of the poem and thus both useful and appropriate and always so, no matter what possibility has been conjectured.

VII

Possible meaning is usually an emanation from the given and in Stevens' poetry often has its source in an image or in some figure meditating or speaking. Possibility that develops from a specific point in the given is a kind of semantic vector with an open but restricted area of meaning—like an angle. Since the given is the ground of the possible, the wordless radial meanings from an image or figure must be conjectured from the statements and the structure of the discourse. When the suggestive force of the given is insufficient, then the poet's customary use for implication of the image or figure must be recalled. In several of Stevens' poems the given offers little or no indication of the nature of "the poem of the idea." The given in "Somnambulisma," for instance, is composed of a scene presented as existing and an image of a bird presented as analogy. The analogy is extended until it has the effect of superseding the thing compared.

"Somnambulisma" begins with a description of a sea, with its waves breaking on a beach and washing back and forth. In the poem, the motion of a bird is depicted, but not as existing in the scene, for the bird is presented as an analogy to wave action on the shore:

9. Joseph Riddel, *The Clairvoyant Eye* (Baton Rouge: Louisiana State University Press, 1965), p. 196.

On an old shore, the vulgar ocean rolls
Noiselessly, noiselessly, resembling a thin bird,
That thinks of settling, yet never settles, on a nest.

The wings keep spreading and yet are never wings.
The claws keep scratching on the shale, the shallow shale,
The sounding shallow, until by water washed away.

The generations of the bird are all
By water washed away. They follow after,
They follow, follow, follow, in water washed away.

(*CP*, 304)

The scene illustrates the title "Somnambulisma," which is derived from Stevens' notion that the natural world is asleep and that where there is no consciousness, there can be no awakening. In this sense, the movement of the ocean is a kind of sleepwalking. This is "the vulgar ocean," one common to all men. Because somnambulism is an unconscious human activity, the ocean can be considered symbolic of the collective unconscious where the natural, the material, merges into the psychic, the human. Precedent can be found in Stevens' poems for the ocean as a symbol of the unconscious, or, as he usually speaks of it, the subconscious. In "Jasmine's Beautiful Thoughts underneath the Willow," subliminal happiness is found in an ocean within the self, an ocean moving as though with the "capricious" repetitions of fugal and choral music. The individuality of love, the poem says, is like "a vivid apprehension":

Of bliss submerged beneath appearance,
In an interior ocean's rocking
Of long, capricious fugues and chorals.   (*CP*, 79)

Among other oceans and seas in Stevens, there is "the veritable ocean" of "The Idea of Order at Key West," which represents the physical universe, in contrast to human consciousness. This is also a possible meaning for the basic image of "Somnambulisma." But the poem's title; the ocean that rolls "noiselessly, noiselessly"; the analogy of the bird; the poem's mention of the lack of a human observer; the word vulgar in its primary sense of general, public, belonging to the people—all point toward the idea of a collective unconsciousness as an appropriate symbolic import for "the vulgar ocean." The birdlike motion of onshore waves may suggest little movements toward consciousness on the edge of the vast unconscious that is itself matter, grasping at the reality that is the shore, trying to settle on it, to rest on it, but continually washed away by flux, by process. But if the ocean is conceived as a scene of the physical universe, then the bird is no more than what is presented—a descriptive analogy for the movements of process, with each particular, each integer, washed away in the wavelike motion of the eternal flux:

> Without this bird that never settles, without
> Its generations that follow in their universe,
> The ocean, falling and falling on the hollow shore,
>
> Would be a geography of the dead: not of that land
> To which they may have gone, but of the place in which
> They lived, in which they lacked a pervasive being,
>
> In which no scholar, separately dwelling,
> Poured forth the fine fins, the gawky beaks, the personalia,
> Which, as a man feeling everything, were his.   (*CP*, 304)

The point of the negative, of "no scholar," is that the unconscious has no observer, that no consciousness sees its somnambulism, or—taking this description to be a scene and nothing more—that the scene is a physical or natural place without human presence. On the other hand, the last stanza can also be taken to mean that no scholar is "separately dwelling," that he holds within him "the vulgar ocean"—the unconscious that he can never see or know—and that in the reality of his existence, he writes his poems, feels his "personalia"—images like the bird moving in analogy to waves on a shore. The phrase, "feeling everything," seems to establish in the mind the reality of the scholar. The scene would be dead, the poem suggests, without the little successive approaches of the unconscious toward reality, which are like waves washed away, like a bird trying to settle, trying to nest in reality—a "hollow shore" because it is not truly solid in itself but a shell of appearance. These are possibilities and when so conceived, they give the poem echoings beyond the immediacy of the discourse—a resonance that is so characteristic of Stevens' great style.[10]

Discussions like this one of the possible in poems, with no comment by Stevens himself, represent no more than a reader's point of view. However, conjecture can be bolstered not only by repetitions of images and ideas from other poems but also by the plain fact that Stevens was very much aware of this double aspect of his art. In one of the "Adagia," he speaks of the given and the possible aspects of an image and reflects that meaning reaches beyond discourse: "The bare image and the image as a symbol are the contrast: the image without meaning and the image as meaning. When the image is used to suggest something else, it is secondary. Poetry as an imaginative thing consists of more than lies on the surface" (*OP*, 161)

The purpose of this examination of "Somnambulisma" is to study possibility in a poem that has a minimum of indicia for inference in its discourse. More than one possibility is noted, for the possible is an area of meaning rather than one certain mean-

---

10. In an early letter, Stevens shows that he was fascinated by an analogy between the movement of mental process and of the sea; he keeps repeating "the mind rolls as the sea rolls" (*L*, 119).

ing. But not just anything that might come to mind is useful; to be credible, explication must be concerned with what is appropriate to the poet's customary usage and to the context of the poem. As the possible is indefinite and almost inexhaustible within its semantic area, variant readings (even by the same critic) are to be expected.

When there is a general agreement about the possible—as there is to some extent about Stevens' color symbolism—then the possible begins to have the effect of a given. It is known as though read, not inferred. Critics concentrate on implications, and since abstraction is inherent in the possible (its logic being inherently inductive), criticism makes the poetry seem more expository than it is to a reader intent on "the poem of the words." However, Stevens' poems continually shed their paraphrase and stand fresh and open without any stinting of their possibilities. From the character of the poetry itself, it is evident that Stevens demanded of a poem, as he said in 1951, "a meaning beyond what its words can possibly say, a sound beyond any giving of the ear, a motion beyond our previous knowledge of feeling" (*OP,* 210).[11]

---

11. Isabel G. MacCaffrey's discussion of the poem of the idea and the poem of the words in "The Ways of Truth in 'Le Monocle de Mon Oncle'" was of great value to me when writing this chapter. See her beautiful and illuminating essay in *WS,* 196–218.

Four

THESE IMAGES REPEAT AND ARE INCREASED

I

Stevens' memories of writing poetry indicate that it was generally a deductive process. Beginning with some slight concept, often an indefinite abstraction, he developed an area of thought into a meditation from which the import of the poem's discourse had its inception. The meditation, however, was only an organizing phase; he did not write a poem in order to tell what he had been thinking. The purpose of his thought was ultimately the poetry he hoped to achieve, he said. And in a letter written two year before the much quoted line, "Poetry is the subject of the poem" (*CP*, 176), he said that "one's subject is always poetry, or should be." By saying poetry is always his subject, he means it is always his object, for, as he explained, "my object in all this is simply to write poetry, keeping it as true as possible to myself and as near as possible to the idea I have in mind" (*L,* 291).[1]

The prelude to the final phase of composition was usually a period of heightened emotion, when the poet enjoyed "bursts of freedom" (*L,* 297) and a release of creative impulse directed by the organizing process of prior thinking into an appropriate flow of words. Along with the language of the poem, its imagery appeared, for poetic imagery has its inception and growth with language. Imagery for Stevens was itself a language that signified by implication.

The fictive circumstance or occasion for a poem's discourse is a kind of containing image itself: the scene of what is said or done in the poem and the raison d'être of the mode of address used by the speaker of the discourse. The scene or incident may be merely implied, as in so many poems that use apostrophe—like "O Florida Venereal Soil" or "Farewell to Florida." For example, "Apostrophe to Vincentine," with its successive views of a protagonist, gives an effect of someone approaching from a distance. There is, for another example, the latent scene of an older man instructing a youth; this is the circumstance of the first poem of "Notes toward a Supreme Fiction" and is implied in the first line, "Begin, ephebe, by perceiving the idea."

In addition to the containing scene or circumstance that is the occasion of a poem, there may be a number of other implied or indefinite scenes, situations, images. The growth of an indefinite image from an abstraction can be surmised from Stevens' account of his plans for the opening of "Notes toward a Supreme Fiction." In explanation of his intention, Stevens said that when he was

1. "Most of the poems that I have written, at least in recent years, have been written in the morning on my way to the office," Stevens said in 1949. He nearly always walked to the office and conjectured that the rhythm of walking may have entered his verse. "I make notes and try to fix things in my mind and then when I arrive at the office arrange these things and, finally, when I am at home in the evening I write the thing out" (*L,* 641).

preparing to write this poem, he had initially thought he would have a definite progression of idea and that the beginning, the first poem, would bear "the caption REFACIMENTO." Then he added that "the first step toward a supreme fiction would be to get rid of all existing fictions." "A thing stands out in clear air better than it does in soot" (*L*, 431). This statement translated into poetry becomes not only the language of the poem but an implicit scene of someone looking at the sun as though for the first time and seeing it as an image of the idea of an objective reality:

> You must become an ignorant man again
> And see the sun again with an ignorant eye.   (*CP*, 380)

The ephebe looking at the sun is a suggested rather than revealed image in the discourse of the poem's implied circumstance, the little scene of an older man instructing a young man.

Undefined situations and almost imperceptible images deepen significance, give density to expository passages. When Stevens was working on "Owl's Clover," he spoke of the utility of unrealized images. "I am thinking of using images that are never fully defined. We constantly use such images: any state of mind is in effect such an image. This is part of the rapidity of thought" (*L*, 319). Three years later, a comment on "The Man with the Blue Guitar," XXV again reveals Stevens' awareness of indefinite images and their part in the "rapidity of thought" while conceiving a poem. "When the imagination is moving rapidly, it identifies things only approximately, and to stop to define them would be to stop altogether" (*L*, 361).

II

The ease with which his writing of a poem often proceeded was, for Stevens, undoubtedly due largely to a mastery of style. In-

trinsic to this style are its continually recurring features.[2] These
elements include not only habitual sentence forms and vocabulary
and the indefinite imagery Stevens mentions as part of the rapidity of thought, but also certain little scenes, certain complex
images, which are like glimpses of situations and occur again and
again. They vary enough to prevent easy recognition as they re-
appear. These images must have come almost instinctively to
Stevens as forms embodying thoughts. And, in accordance with
the general development of his poetry, they seem to carry more
and more abstract import as they recur. For example, as early as
1905, Stevens saw that someone expressing in a letter his feeling
for another person could be compared to a musician playing an
instrument, expressing feeling in music. The transition was easy
from this simile to "Music is feeling, then, not sound" (*CP*, 90).
Thus the image of someone playing on an instrument became a
depiction of an individual apprehending his emotions. Later the
player on an instrument began to represent the idea of the self
realizing its individual experience of the world, as in "The Man
with the Blue Guitar." Stevens' proclivity for expanding his symbolic references can be illustrated by tracing several recurrences of
the image of the player and his instrument.

In one of those fragments that his wife saved from his early
letters to her, Stevens endowed the image with the basic meaning
it had for him: "I thought today that our letters were like some
strange instrument full of delicate and endearing music—music just
a little haunting, on which we played for each other in turn" (*L,*

2. For an example of such repetition, see "Variations on a Nude" in
my book, *Stevens' Poetry of Thought* (Baltimore: Johns Hopkins Press,
1966). See also Northrop Frye's discussion of Stevens' recurrent concepts,
"Wallace Stevens and the Variation Form," in *Literary Theory and Structure: Essays in Honor of William K. Wimsatt,* ed. Frank Brady, John Palmer,
and Martin Price (New Haven, Yale University Press, 1973).

81). The enchanting echo of this simile occurred seven years later when Peter Quince said:

> And thus it is that what I feel,
> Here in this room, desiring you,
>
> Thinking of your blue-shadowed silk,
> Is music. (*CP*, 90)

The image was so indigenous to Stevens that after the passing of ten more years, the music of the poet at the piano in "Mozart, 1935" is still feeling, but unlike "the strain/Waked in the elders by Susanna," the feeling now is "angry fear" and "besieging pain," for this is the era of the Great Depression: "The snow is falling/And the streets are full of cries" (*CP*, 132).

In "The Man with the Blue Guitar," the symbolic implication of the player on an instrument has developed into an idea of the individual making what he can of the world with his instrument, his conceiving mind. Stevens noted what he had in mind on the dust jacket of the trade edition of that poem: "Although the blue guitar is a symbol of the imagination, it is used most often simply as a reference to the individuality of the poet, meaning by the poet any man of imagination." And, from the poetry itself, it is evident that by the imagination Stevens often means the process that gives each person his version of the reality he encounters, for the world in his individual sense of it has the singularity of his own unique personality. Yet what else can the world be than what he thinks it is and says it is?

> And things are as I think they are
> And say they are on the blue guitar. (*CP*, 180)

In this vein, the poem reflects the idea that what is seen is changed only in respect to the transfer from the world outside to the inner world of the mind:

Yet nothing changed, except the place

Of things as they are and only the place
As you play them, on the blue guitar.   (*CP,* 167)

There is a chaos of many things to be experienced, and the
music of the guitar brings disparate sights, sounds, and objects
into the order that is the apperceptive unity of the inner self. As
Stevens says of the poem that describes a storm and the clearing
of the weather, "It is like reason addressing itself to chaos and
brings it to bear: puts it in the confines of focus" (*L,* 791):

I know my lazy, leaden twang
Is like the reason in a storm;

And yet it brings the storm to bear.
I twang it out and leave it there.   (*CP,* 169)

In the fourth poem of "Esthétique du Mal," the import of the
player on an instrument has grown even vaster, more abstract.
"B.," the figure at the piano, makes a transparence, the poem de-
clares, and in that transparence "we heard music, made music" or,
to paraphrase, we undergo our experiences, create our experiences.
"B." is Be and the transparence that "B." or Being makes is the
human consciousness:

When B. sat down at the piano and made
A transparence in which we heard music, made music,
In which we heard transparent sounds, did he play
All sorts of notes?   (*CP,* 316)

The question posed concerns the idea of human experience. The
poem asks, in this musical analogy, if experience is heterogenous, in
that it is a scattering into many minds, each conceiving separately its
separate world. Were there all sorts of notes, as in a "Livre de Toutes
Sortes de Fleurs d'après Nature" of the fourth poem's first line?

> . . . Or did he play only one
> In an ecstasy of its associates,
> Variations in the tones of a single sound,
> The last, or sounds so single they seemed one?   (*CP*, 316)

Or is human experience a unity, an expression of the oneness of nature, whose unity is manifested in the unthinking sensuous life of the human body, with each single body only a variation on that unity?

By its question, the poem presents two possibilities for the nature of experience: an idea of many separate intelligences and their individualized experience of the world and an idea of the unity of experience by the agency of the body, rooted in the unity of nature. These divergent conceptions bring to mind the Apollonian-Dionysiac cleavage of Nietzsche's *The Birth of Tragedy*, a book that discusses the philosophic implications of music. In Stevens' poem, the notion of a diversity of individuals with separate frames of experience is the "book of all kinds of flowers after nature," as the first line of the poem implies. "All sorts of flowers," the second line repeats. "That's the sentimentalist." Nietzsche says that when there is an intrusion of the dreaming, gazing Apollonian individuality into the primordial Dionysiac oneness, it is as if "a sentimental trait of nature were coming to the fore, as though nature were bemoaning the fact of her fragmentation, her decomposition into separate individuals." In contrast, the Dionysiac impulse is "to sink back into the original oneness of nature."[3]

This poem illustrates one form of composition that Stevens often uses: a presentation of certain recurrent images that are like partly developed situations separted by little more than ellipses. In this poem, the image of the player on an instrument is succeeded without connective comment by another thematic image:

3. Trans. Francis Golffing (Garden City, N.Y.: Doubleday, 1956), p. 27.

the lover and his beloved, described as the Spaniard and the rose. The Spaniard is a Dionysiac figure—a personification of the sensuous life of the body, who rescues as his beloved the reality known by intuition. He is like the poet in the "Adagia": "A poet looks at the world as a man looks at a woman" (*OP*, 165). He would take for his own his immediate sensuous contact with reality and never mistake for this physical involvement with the real the Apollonian array of concepts commonly available through the intellect:

> And then that Spaniard of the rose, itself
> Hot-hooded and dark-blooded, rescued the rose
> From nature, each time he saw it, making it,
> As he saw it, exist in his own especial eye.
> Can we conceive of him as rescuing less,
> As muffing the mistress for her several maids,
> As foregoing the nakedest passion for barefoot
> Philandering?   (*CP*, 316)

It is also typical of Stevens' mode of composition that, after presenting his ideas by means of the three images—the book of all sorts of flowers, the player on an instrument, the lover of reality— he concludes the poem with an expository passage that explains his bias for the body and its immediate, unthinking, sensory response. There he reflects that human misfortune is not due to the sentimental notion of individual intelligences, each living in its separate world. Our misfortune is caused by the nature of mind, which must transform reality into conceptions, and conceptions are inherently fictive. Yet such fictions are the very being of the mind. The genius of the body, its physical reality that is part of the reality of the world, is wasted by the mind that can realize only its own concepts:

> . . . the genius of
> The mind, which is our being, wrong and wrong,

> The genius of the body, which is our world,
> Spent in the false engagements of the mind.   (*CP*, 316–17)

The lover and beloved image in an earlier poem, "The Sense of the Sleight-of-Hand Man," anticipates the meaning of the image in "Esthétique du Mal," IV. The poem describes the spontaneous occurrence of intuition of events in the natural world and then implies that only the body in its physical life can touch the reality of the world:

> It may be that the ignorant man, alone,
> Has any chance to mate his life with life
> That is the sensual, pearly spouse, the life
> That is fluent in even the wintriest bronze.   (*CP*, 222)

"The sensual, pearly spouse," like the rose that is itself "hot-hooded and dark-blooded" and rescued from nature, is an anima figure projected as the reality the self longs to realize. And the ignorant man is a version of the physical intuitive self, like the Spaniard of the rose.

III

With its profusion of tropes and persons and situations, and its inexhaustible idea that becomes many ideas, Stevens' poetry gives an impression of prodigality. This ostensible heterogeneity receives an inner consonance from a continual repetition of certain scenes, thoughts, images. Because there is such variety in their presentation, the frequent recurrence of these components is never obtrusive. Veiled repetition of this kind is a factor in the unity of a poetry that issues, evidently, from lavish inventiveness.

For instance, in the first part of "Two Tales of Liadoff," there are two major images: Liadoff at the piano and people crowding into a rocket and lighting the fuse. The first, plainly enough, is a version of the player on an instrument. The second, however, seems unique in Stevens' work and yet may be considered a variation, although an anomolous one, of the Stevens trope that presents consciousness as an interior light, a burning candle, a sparkle, a glitter. The rocket is not easily recognized as a variant of this image of consciousness. It is striking and appears to be without precedent, although there is one other rocket in a Stevens poem. The Chinese rocket in "Carnet de Voyage," written in 1909, apparently was a falling star, and its function was to serve as an example of brilliant but brief illumination.[4] In "Two Tales of Liadoff," the rocket describes a soaring experience of a concert of music:

> Do you remember how the rocket went on
> And on, at night, exploding finally
> In an ovation of resplendent forms?   (*CP*, 346)

A rocket as an image of consciousness is not as original as it might seem. The image and its idea had already appeared in Henri Bergson's *Creative Evolution*. There the development of consciousness as an aspect of the evolution of life from matter was illustrated by the action of a rocket ascending through the ashes of prior rockets, with the creative-decreative process of this evolution like "the fiery path torn by the last rocket of a fireworks display through the black cinders of the spent rockets that are falling dead."[5] Later in the same book, consciousness is a rocket with an explosive force that enables matter to transcend itself. "Consciousness,

---

4. Stevens had the rocket image in mind around this time. A letter of November 26, 1945, expresses his wish to give an ovation like that of a rocket: "I should like to take a trip through the air and go several thousand miles straight up and there explode into no end of stars, which from a distance would read, in Spanish, 'regards to Pompilio'" (*L*, 520).
5. Trans. Arthur Mitchell (New York: Modern Library, 1944), pp. 273–74. The second quotation is on pages 284–85.

or supra-consciousness, is the name for the rocket whose extinguished fragments fall back as matter; consciousness, again, is the name for that which subsists of the rocket itself, passing through the fragments and lighting them up into organisms."

Stevens' version of the image resembles Bergson's, except that from the exalted heights of musical experience the people descend into their normal subjectivity, and in Bergson the spent fragments of rockets descend as matter. The mind's interior discourse, its unintended flow of thought or, as the poem presents it, what the people said as they heard Liadoff's "haunted arpeggios," is repeated by Liadoff. The "incredible colors" of his music are an enhanced version of their rocket—"ex, ex and ex and out." Stevens' lines suggest an idea of the interaction of life and art, for what the people say when they fall back as themselves is transformed by Liadoff into music in the sense that art, in all its transcendent glory, follows from and reflects the inner life of humanity. The image of the rocket in Stevens' poem is a depiction of the heightened experience of an audience at a concert, with the resplendent forms of the music conceived as transmuted into an ovation of intense feeling in the minds of the audience, and the music itself an emanation from human thought and emotion:

> Ovation on ovation of large blue men
> In pantaloons of fire and of women hatched,
> Like molten citizens of the vacuum?
>
> Do you remember the children there like wicks,
> That constantly sparkled their small gold? The town
> Had crowded into the rocket and touched the fuse.
>
> (*CP*, 346)

The image gains significance and resonance when the sparkling light of the rocket is associated with other versions of Stevens' basic image of the light of consciousness: "the scholar of one candle," "the glitter of a being," "the spirit's diamond coronal," "a glitter that is a life." However, the image must always be seen in its context. Many uses of the image of light or gleam or glitter occur in a context that confers other meanings.

IV

The other major image of "Two Tales of Liadoff" is more complex than the simple instance of the player on an instrument, which it seems to be:

That night, Liadoff, a long time after his death,
At a piano in a cloud sat practicing,
On a black piano practiced epi-tones.   (*CP,* 346)

This scene depicting a ghost playing a piano in a cloud is formed of several components that recur elsewhere in other guises and, in a sense, can be considered a cluster of images. When abstracted, the images in this cluster are the figure in a cloud, the player on an instrument, the ghost or spirit as artist. Stevens' recurring images are given a deeper relationship by the fairly consistent significance they embody in each of their appearances. For example, the figure in a cloud suggests the idea of an intuition or an influence or sudden inspiration, as in these instances: the Indian who "struck / Out of his cloud and from his sky," in "The Cuban Doctor"; "a ghost that inhabits a cloud," in "The Lack of Repose"; and "the angel in his cloud," in "Notes toward a Supreme Fiction"—a figure who also plays an instrument in a cloud.

The second of the images abstracted from the cluster, the player on an instrument, is Liadoff, a real figure in the history of music. Instead of representing the idea of the self conceiving the world in its individual way, as the image so often suggests, in this poem it stands for the continual existence of Liadoff's music. Although the image of Liadoff at his piano does not appear per se in the second of the "Two Tales of Liadoff," its implicit presence supports the major theme: the idea that the transformation of the work of art—the music, the poem—into the inner experience of the auditor, the reader, is a kind of violence that occurs when the music is heard, or the poem read, and thus becomes a part of organic life. In Stevens' words: "It is/The instant of the change that was the poem." The effect of this change from the abstraction that is the objective work of art to the experience of the live creature is like an inversion from ghost to living person:

> As if Liadoff no longer remained a ghost
> And, being straw, turned green, lived backward, shared
>
> The fantastic fortune of fantastic blood, . . .   (*CP*, 347)

The ghost is what remains of Liadoff after his death—his music that still exists in its notation, its objective state. The ghost is another of Stevens' recurring images and establishes itself by recurrence as a symbol of the work that can survive the artist. The image first occurs in "The Weeping Burgher," which implies that to appear as a ghost is to be known by one's poems. It is in the calcined heart of poetry—its oft-burned center—that the poet expends his burning feelings, sheds his tears. And he asks that if he appears among those still living in his apprehending them—"burning in me still," perhaps the poets who still kindle his feelings—that his poems stand in his stead and exemplify the style to which he aspires:

> Permit that if as ghost I come
> Among the people burning in me still,
> I come as belle design
> Of foppish line.
>
> And I, then, tortured for old speech,
> A white of wildly woven rings;

I, weeping in a calcined heart,
My hands such sharp, imagined things.   (*CP*, 61)

Old speech that is "a white of wildly woven rings" is the poetic diction of the great poets. The hands in the last line are a depiction of the expressive gesturing language that he hopes his poems may be. The image also has connotations for the idea of creative activity.

Two years after this poem appeared in *Poetry,* Stevens wrote Harriet Monroe that Genevieve Taggard had been speaking of a group of his poems just published in *Poetry* and told him "there was an impression abroad that the poems were hideous ghosts of myself" (*L*, 222–23). Stevens' comment was "it may be." And it may be that the witticism played with the ghost image in "The Weeping Burgher."[6]

The beautiful image in "A Postcard from the Volcano" of the poetry of one who once lived in the mansion or cultural structure that is a civilization—"a spirit storming in blank walls"—defines for the poets of a later day, the "children, / Still weaving budded aureoles," their sense of the passionate life of one who seems to survive in his poetry.

The twenty-ninth poem of "Like Decorations in a Nigger Cemetery" is another instance of the same kind of symbolic meaning for the ghost image:

Choke every ghost with acted violence,
Stamp down the phosphorescent toes, tear off
The spittling tissues tight across the bones.
The heavy bells are tolling rowdy-dow.   (*CP*, 155)

---

6. Stevens wrote in the flyleaf of his daughter Holly's copy of *The Collected Poems*: "Ghosts that dally with life's savor upon their lips." See Milton J. Bates, "Stevens' Books at the Huntington: An Annotated Checklist," *The Wallace Stevens Journal* 3, nos. 1 and 2 (1979): 30.

From Stevens' own explanation of these lines, a ghost here seems to stand for the poems of poets who might impose their character on that of his own. The symbolic violence of his rejection of these ghosts, he suggests, is that of his effort to retain his own identity and of his desire to write a poetry based on reality rather than literature. In Stevens' words, "Paraphrased, this means: cast out the spirit that you have inherited for one of your own, for one based on reality. Thus, the bells are not ghostly, nor do they make phosphorescent sounds, so to speak. They are heavy and 'are tolling rowdy-dow'" (*L*, 349). No longer does Stevens wish to appear "as belle design/Of foppish line" like the weeping burgher of the *Harmonium* period. It is another decade, and now he aspires to the heavy tolling of the real world, as opposed to the phosphorescence of literary mannerism.

In another poem concerned with literary influence, "The Lack of Repose," a ghost in a cloud represents the poetry of a poet who is the precursor or literary ancestor and whose book speaks to the creative faculties of his successor.[7] It is not the ghost of romance but one that addresses the real person, an "Andrew Jackson Something," who will in turn become a precursor himself:

It is a ghost that inhabits a cloud,
But a ghost for Andrew, not lean, catarrhal
And pallid. It is the grandfather he liked,
With an understanding compounded by death

And the associations beyond death, even if only
Time. What a thing it is to believe that
One understands, in the intense disclosures
Of a parent in the French sense.   (*CP*, 303)

In "Notes toward a Supreme Fiction," there is a variation on

7. All this poetry about influences and predecessors brings to mind Harold Bloom's *The Anxiety of Influence* (New York: Oxford, 1973).

the image of a ghost in a cloud. Here the ghost is another kind of imaginary spiritual being, an angel playing a stringed instrument in a luminous cloud. The figure suggests the idea of a muse and thus seems to be a personification of poetry, for the angel "Plucks on his strings to pluck abysmal glory." And, as if to bring out this understanding of the image, the poet himself asks if it is not he that sits in the cloud plucking his strings, asks if the experience of "expressible bliss" is not his, rather than that of the angel:

> Is it he or is it I that experience this?
> Is it I then that keep saying there is an hour
> Filled with expressible bliss, in which I have
>
> No need, am happy, forget need's golden hand, . . .

(*CP*, 404–5)

The angel plucking an instrument in a cloud is a cluster of the same images that can be abstracted from the depiction of Liadoff in a cloud at his piano. These images, if reduced or abstracted to their basic pattern, hold a relationship when repeated that is more schematic than visual. A basic recurring pattern like that of a figure playing an instrument is thus a kind of schema.

In the growth of a poem, when its idea was developed into its specific discourse, Stevens seems to have turned instinctively to patterns of images or schemata that were appropriate to his ideas. Examples of these schemata are the reader scanning a book, someone lying or tossing on a bed, a person or persons in a boat, people seated at a table, someone looking in a glass, a figure on a stage, someone seeking or longing for another, a hand holding or elevating something, people in a procession or parade, and an interior figure—one in a cavern or crevice or cage.

As the schemata kept occurring to him, they apparently became embodiments of certain basic concepts of the human condition. For example, an image of a hand presented for display, usually grasping something, appeared in poems from *Harmonium* to *The Auroras of Autumn*, and when Stevens' Cuban correspondent wrote in a letter that "a hand, in a black glove, holds a novel by Camus," Stevens recognized its similarity to his own symbol and quoted the passage from the letter in "The Novel" (*L*, 617). He had used the hand to symbolize the mind holding its experience of place in "O Florida Venereal Soil" and as the creative imagination in "The Hand as a Being." In "The Novel," the hand represents the mind realizing a work of art that spreads its influence over a room and the human circumstance of the poem.

The major component of a schema is usually a human figure, or, if it is not, then it is symbolic of a human feature or trait—like the serpent in "The Bagatelles the Madrigals." In this poem, the serpent represents the human mind "baffled/By the trash of life," mulling its bitterness in its crevice of earth, the inner darkness of the body, the camera obscura where thought occurs. In the course of his poetry, these recurring patterns of elements appear among many other images that show themselves for one time only. The persistence of the schemata, their continually echoing quality, infuses them with significance that an image in isolation might not have. Unhampered by the developmental character of narrative, the schemata are adapted to the indefinite and hypothetical nature of thought in these poems. And the effect of the repetition of these little scenes is to enhance the unity of Stevens' poetry.

Five

 # ONE LOOKS AT THE SEA

I

"Possibly the unity between any man's poems is the unity of his nature," Stevens wrote Latimer in a comment on the development of his poetry (*L*, 294). Evidence of the unity of his own nature can be seen in the repetition of ideas, images, and rhetorical forms over all his years of writing. The scenes or situations that recur in various forms, the basic patterns of which can be abstracted as schemata, are an important component of the consonance of Stevens' poetry. A schema of one of these images or scenes is its recurring configuration of certain coordinate elements.

A figure on a shore either looking at or thinking of the sea is an example of such an image. The sea, the person, the shore may vary considerably, but the interrelationship remains fairly constant. In several remarkable poems, this scene is the focal circumstance, and it appears at every phase of his development. This schema or any

other may carry from other contexts symbolic value that adheres
to its repeated elements. Its meaning deepened and schematic
character tightened by repetition, the figure by the sea exempli-
fies the function of schematic imagery in Stevens' poetry. The
essence of this scene is a depiction of mind, of imagination on
the edge of reality, one of many representations of Stevens' constant theme: the interaction of mind and world. The following
survey of the appearance of this schema may reveal something of
the many concepts of a representation that impinge on the thought
of the poet when he is engaged in the work of composition.

II

The schema of person, sea, and shore in some poems conveys
presentiment, suggests a tragic circumstance. Considerable correspondence of idea and symbolic details relates these poems; their
thematic correlations, their common portent, compose them into
a group. Most are rather early or late poems; the reappearance at
wide intervals of the schema with this common sense of fore-
boding reflects the unexplainable reverberations of the poet's life
of temperament and thought. In most of the poems thus related, the sea is an image of time and change, with the traditional
connotations for disintegration or mortality. It is "the assassin's
scene," according to a version of the schema in "Esthétique du
Mal" (*CP*, 324).

The figure on a shore makes its initial appearance in the first
line of a sonnet published in the *Harvard Monthly* in 1899: "I
strode along my beaches like a sea." The poem echoes conventional *fin de siècle* mood poems. Yet, when it is compared with
the achievement of his last years, the beginnings of that achievement can be glimpsed:

I strode along my beaches like a sea,
The sand before me stretching firm and fair

No inland darkness cast its shadow there
And my long step was gloriously free.
The careless wind was happy company.   (*Buttel*, 12)

The poet and his world are in accord as the poem begins. Then the
tone changes into the mood of presentiment that the schema reflects in several later poems:

Yet as I moved I felt a deep despair
And wonder of the thoughts that came to me.

For to my face the deep wind brought the scent
Of flowers I could not see upon the strand;
And in the sky a silent cloud was blent
With dreams of my soul's stillness; and the sand
That had been nought to me, now trembled far
In mystery beneath the evening star.   (*Buttel*, 12)

This little allegory of a young man striding the beach of his
existence, the sand before him "stretching firm and fair," is a
precursor of "The Auroras of Autumn," II, in which a man walking an empty beach "turns blankly on the sand" (*CP*, 412). The
mood indicated in the great poem of his last years seems an aus-
tere echo of "the deep despair/And wonder" of the walker in
the early poem. In the first poem, "no inland darkness cast its
shadow," and the inland darkness foreshadows the impending
darkness of the later poem: "a darkness gathers though it does
not fall." Both poems end with an ominous symbol in the sky.
In the early poem, "a silent cloud was blent/With dreams of my
soul's stillness." The aurora borealis of the later poem symbolizes
"a tragic and desolate background," according to Stevens (*L*,
852). From the summer evening of the Harvard sonnet to the late
fall evening of "The Auroras of Autumn," II, a lifetime inter-
venes, and still the scene of the man walking the beach is a tableau
of a time of life and a presentiment of its close.

"The Auroras of Autumn," II is also faintly reminiscent of an entry in Stevens' journal for August 24, 1902, written after a walk on the seashore. Features in the journal entry that anticipate the grave poem of his late years are the long beach stretching before him, the vivid lights in the sky, the lowering clouds, and the declining sun. His early account had an air of despondency. He spoke of "the severity of the prospect" and said that "walking over the beach under this lowering sky was like stepping into a cavern" (*L*, 60). Faint echoes of such early impressions in his late poem indicate a persisting affectability, a consistency of mind rather than a recollection.

Another Harvard sonnet with ideas that recur in later poems suggests the concept of a human presence on a shore, but this time by a negation. In "Cathedrals are not built along the sea" a human structure substitutes for the human figure (*Buttel*, 17–18). "Cathedrals are not built along the sea" because the sea is too real, too much of a threat to the products of the human imagination. The poem contrasts the life and works of the mind with natural events and forces; cathedrals and their content stand for the world of human conception, and the sea stands for external reality.

The idea that the sea is a symbol of the menace that time and process pose to the human imagination and its creations recurs in "The Doctor of Geneva." Although the churches of the city of Geneva, like the cathedrals of the Harvard sonnet, are not built along the sea, the doctor realizes that they are not therefore protected from the processes symbolized by the sea. Prophetic intimations of the waste of time in the movement of the waves puts his mind in a ferment, like the turmoil of water before him:

> Which yet found means to set his simmering mind
> Spinning and hissing with oracular
> Notations of the wild, the ruinous waste,
>
> Until the steeples of his city clanked and sprang
> In an unburgherly apocalypse. (*CP*, 24)

The doctor's feeling of presentiment is described with an ironic amusement characteristic of other Stevens poems that show the individual will at odds with universal process.[1]

The idea of flux that dismays the doctor of Geneva occurs to him by analogy. As he looks at the sea, he surmises the ruin of his city and its churches, for he finds the water before him to be "the wild, the ruinous waste." The word "waste" offers its double meaning, and the sea with its incessant fluctuation becomes an image of continual and universal change.

When the schema reappears in "The Man with the Blue Guitar," XXVII, the figure is any man and the shore any place where man exists. The sea of time and change advances on that shore like the coming of winter. The sea's association with winter darkens its tenor, gives it the grave connotations that Stevens' poems hold for images of reality as flux:

> It is the sea that whitens the roof.
> The sea drifts through the winter air.
>
> It is the sea that the north wind makes.
> The sea is in the falling snow.
>
> This gloom is the darkness of the sea.   (CP, 179)

This idea of a winter sea and its "iceberg settings" is a mild

---

1. See "Bantams in Pine-Woods," for instance. Santayana explains the dismay of a civilized, dogmatic mind like that of the doctor of Geneva's at the idea of universal natural process. He is speaking of the "cosy world" of books, of dogma. "The civilized mind is still very much more at home in such a cosy world than in the universal flux of nature, which not only opens material immeasurable abysses on every side of our human nest, but threatens us with an indefinite flux in our own being, in our habits, institutions, affections, and in the very grammer and categories of our thought." It almost seems that "The Doctor of Geneva" is a poetic rendering of this passage. See Santayana, *Winds of Doctrine and Platonism and the Spiritual Life* (New York: Harper, 1967), p. 281.

preliminary for the mood invoked by the arctic sea of "Page from a Tale," a poem of the same great somber period as "The Auroras of Autumn." The sea of ice suggesting a time of universal impending disaster is indicated as a symbol by a passage that compares the sea to an image in a dream: "The sea was a sea he dreamed./Yet Hans lay wide awake." Hans, the figure on the shore, sitting in solitude by his driftwood fire, sees a great ship frozen in the ice. It is night and the monstrous stars are portents of destruction:

> The great ship, Balayne, lay frozen in the sea.
> The one-foot stars were couriers of its death
> To the wild limits of its habitation.   (*CP*, 421)

The great ship, Balayne, like the cathedrals of the Harvard sonnet and the city of churches in "The Doctor of Geneva," is a symbol of social and cultural order. Hans, the figure on a shore in "Page from a Tale," looks at an ocean that represents a grimmer and more imminent apocalypse than that in "The Doctor of Geneva." The transformation of the sun and the giant stars as portents of annihilation bear a visual and conceptual relationship to the northern lights of "The Auroras of Autumn," II. But unlike those symbols of "a tragic and desolate background," these are also symbols of an unknown reality. The men on the ship go out at dawn "to walk ashore" with the little lights of man's limited vision to confront the new reality.[2]

III

When the sea of the schema appears to be a symbolic reference to a harmonious natural world, then the figure by the sea is

2. Another possibility for this poem is vividly described by James Baird, who sees it as an apocalyptic vision of the atomic age. See Baird, *The Dome and the Rock* (Baltimore: Johns Hopkins Press, 1968), pp. 113–16.

presented as though at ease and indigenous there. In two seashore poems of *Harmonium*, "Hibiscus on the Sleeping Shore" and "Fabliau of Florida" (one a daytime and one a nighttime seascape), the mind contemplates the sea in accordance with its nature, as a moth rests on a flower or as a ship may sail out over the water. Twenty years after it was written, Stevens said that "Fabliau of Florida" was a poem he particularly liked. "It is not the sense of a poem of that kind that counts, because it does not really have a great deal of sense; it is the feeling of the words and the reaction and images that the words create" (*L*, 341).

About the time he spoke so favorably of "Fabliau of Florida," he was writing "Variations on a Summer Day," a group of poems in which the essence was also suggested rather than said. This group of poems assumes, too, that the mind is indigenous to the world, although the world seems as incomprehensible as ever to Stevens. "In a world permanently enigmatical," he said of these impressions of a summer day on the coast of Maine, "to hear and see agreeable things involves something more than mere imagism" (*L*, 346). An implication of nearly all these poems is that they are the immediate reflections of someone by the sea.[3] Some are simple spontaneous responses like the first one, in which the imperative makes it more intense than "mere imagism" and hints at an inner dialogue:

> Say of the gulls that they are flying
> In light blue air over dark blue sea.　　　　　　　(*CP*, 232)

Other poems of the series are highly elliptical. The second, for instance, is a statement without a verb, in which ellipses must be

---

3. Edward Butscher sees all three line poems of "Variations on a Summer Day" as implicative of a scene of a man on a shore. See Butscher, "Wallace Stevens' Neglected Fugue: 'Variations on a Summer Day,'" *Twentieth Century Literature* 19 (1973): 153–64.

filled in by inference from subtle implication. Here there is a latent analogy between the sound and movement of water over rock ("a repetition of unconscious things") and the flow of the poet's unconscious creativity, evident in his verbal inventiveness:

A music more than a breath, but less
Than the wind, sub-music like sub-speech,
A repetition of unconscious things.   (*CP*, 232)

This music is the sound of water on the rocky shore—not quite music, just as the activity of the mind emerging from the subliminal matrix of language, but still indefinite verbally, is not quite speech. This sub-music issues from rock and water spontaneously, like the rudiment of an unformulated poem issuing from the poet's creative unconscious:

Letters of rock and water, words
Of the visible elements and of ours.   (*CP*, 232)

An affinity of man with the natural world—prefigured by this analogy of the sounds of the natural world and the words of the poet—is given metaphorical definition in the fifth poem:

The leaves of the sea are shaken and shaken.
There was a tree that was a father,
We sat beneath it and sang our songs.   (*CP*, 233)

Stevens had already thought of the dominant metaphor of this poem many years earlier. In 1902, he wrote in his journal: "When I sit on the shore and listen to the waves they only suggest wind in tree tops" (*L*, 59). In the poem, the wave also brings to mind wind in the top of a tree and the poet sits beneath that imagined tree to write his poem, knowing that he is a child of the natural world and realizing the sea as his symbol for that world. Thirteen years later, a postcard revived the idea of the paternity he had felt on the Maine coast, but this pictured seacoast was Irish—"The Irish Cliffs of Moher":

> This is not landscape, full of the somnambulations
> Of poetry
>
> And the sea. This is my father or, maybe,
> It is as he was,
>
> A likeness, one of the race of fathers: earth
> And sea and air.   (*CP*, 502)

Usually the reality that is earth and sea and air is felt by Stevens to suggest a mother rather than a father. As early as 1921, the sea itself was personified as woman in "Infanta Marina." "Two Versions of the Same Poem" carries this sense of the world mother to its ultimate conception. At the opening of this poem, the sea is "insolid rock," the fundamental reality that supports being. Standing by the sea, the figure turns "once more" to question the place of mind in the world, and the implication is that man continually asks what is the relation of the human mind to the material world:

> Once more he turned to that which could not be fixed.
> By the sea, insolid rock, stentor, and said: . . .   (*CP*, 353)

His question, addressed to one who sails the sea of reality as process, considers that sea the amniotic fluid of the cosmic mother. He asks if there is a fetal creature immersed in the symbolic ocean, the human self who cannot see through his own conceptions to the reality encompassing him:

> Lascar, is there a body, turbulent
> With time, in wavering water lies, swollen
>
> With thought, through which it cannot see?   (*CP*, 354)

In part II, the sea becomes "the human ocean" and its waves the generations of human life. This poem combines the schema of the figure on a shore with that of the figure on an elevation. Old John Zeller, Stevens' great-grandfather, stands on his hill (perhaps the mound of his grave), contemplating the cyclic living and dying of men. From this elevation of thought, he conjectures that the succession of human generations and human experience, with its "ocean of watery images," would wish to escape the material flux—the "cadaverous undulations" of the cosmic mother.

IV

The schema may be the central vision of a poem or it may be merely glimpsed, as when the sun is compared to "Walt Whitman walking along a ruddy shore" (CP, 150), or when "the philosophers' man" of "Asides on the Oboe" mutters his milky lines by the seaside (CP, 250). The frequency of occurrence of the schemata is evidence of their importance as elements of Stevens' customary mode of writing poetry. Apparently, his thought in an early stage of composition often moved into the wonted complex of a schema. Schemata supply illustration to essays as well as to poems: "Take, for example, a beach extending as far as the eye can reach, bordered, on the one hand, by trees and, on the other, by the sea" (NA, 71). This version of the schema from "Three Academic Pieces" indicates the presence of a person by the eye reaching as far as it can. The person here, as in other instances of this schema, is the observer of the natural world, and what the eye observes is the resemblance created by the light and color of shore, sea, and sky. The scene depicts, as Stevens says, his thesis that resemblance is "one of the significant components of the structure of reality." Depiction of an idea, often with only vestigial evidence of the thought thus embodied, is characteristic of the way Stevens presented his meditations in poetry.

One of the ideas indicated by several occurrences of this schema is the Cartesian notion that the mind exists beside and separate from the reality before it. In "Notes toward a Supreme Fiction," the idea is set forth quite plainly: "Adam/In Eden was the father of Descartes" and "we live in a place/That is not our own and, much more, not ourselves" (*CP*, 383). The human figure beside the sea, which symbolizes reality in flux or the reality of the natural world, holds in implication a depiction of subjectivity on the brink of reality.

This view of the mind as near and yet distinct from the environing world is the theme of the opening of "The Idea of Order at Key West." The implicit scene is that of a woman singing as she walks beside the ocean.[4] The singer may be taken as symbol of the conceiving mind or as an image of the poet's inventive faculty. The sea stands for the reality of the world, as the poem makes clear, although its restless movement suggests the tragedy of human existence:

> The ever-hooded, tragic-gestured sea
> Was merely a place by which she walked to sing.   (*CP*, 129)

4. Although it is usually a man, in several poems a woman becomes the figure by the sea. The mistress of the philosophers—wanton, beautiful, fecund, like a personfication of creativity or, to use the traditional term, a sort of muse—offers inspiration on the seashore:

> From whose being by starlight, on sea-coast,
> The innermost good of their seeking
> Might come in the simplest of speech.   (*CP*, 26–27)

There is a similarity of concept between the muse of the philosophers and the figure in Stevens' ode to the creative imagination, "To the One of Fictive Music" whose music, like that of the singer at Key West, "separates us from the wind and sea" (*CP*, 87). Another idea of woman as the figure by the sea is that of "woman on the shore" in "Blue Buildings in the Summer Air" (*CP*, 217). Like most anima figures, she suggests the instinctive life of the unconscious, especially the erotic impulse, in accordance with the traditional image of the siren lying by the sea.

This is one of those Stevens poems in which the flow of thought is altered as it progresses. After its three opening stanzas, the thought is modified in the long transitional stanza leading into the climactic fifth stanza, where the thought is further modified to something very close to idealism. The sixth stanza alters again the flow of thought, and the concluding stanza is an envoi of sorts.

The transitional fourth stanza is somewhat elliptical. "If it was only the dark voice of the sea," the poem says, to show that the singer is more than a mere earthen vessel of song, "but it was more than that." Then, to modify the Cartesian conception of the opening repeated in this stanza—with its placing of human voices beside the meaningless sounds of water and wind—the poem continues to insist that it was more than human song in its magnificent setting of sea and sky. What is more will be declared in the fifth stanza, with its evocation of the poignancy of human feeling and of the inexorable interiority of individual experience:

> . . . But it was more than that,
> More even than her voice, and ours, among
> The meaningless plungings of water and the wind,
> Theatrical distances, bronze shadows heaped
> On high horizons, mountainous atmospheres
> Of sky and sea. (*CP*, 129)

In a comment on this poem, Stevens indicated that its meaning was associated in his mind with a phrase of Bishop George Berkeley's. "In THE IDEA OF ORDER AT KEY WEST life has ceased to be a matter of chance. It may be that every man introduces his own order into the life about him and that the idea of order in general is simply what Bishop Berkeley might have called a fortuitous concourse of personal orders. But still there is order" (*L*, 293). The phrase "a fortuitous concourse of personal orders" does not reflect Berkeley's idealism any more than does Stevens' poem.[5] However, Stevens' comment indicates an intent to hold in his poem a philosophic meaning. It is at least possible that, having Berkeley in mind, the thought in his poem tended toward philosophic idealism. It is in the fifth stanza that there is a strain of idealism. The passage is deepened by a recognition that the scene of a woman singing and realizing a world by her song is a complex of two of Stevens' schemata. Not only is the singer the figure by the sea; the woman creating her own individual experience of the world in her song is a version of the player on an instrument. In accordance with the usual import of this schema, her instrument, her voice, suggests the idea of an individual conceiving mind, and her song symbolizes the flow of formulation that constitutes experience, with its unique sense of things and succession of events:

> She was the single artificer of the world
> In which she sang. And when she sang, the sea,
> Whatever self it had, became the self
> That was her song, for she was the maker.   (*CP*, 129)

In the next stanza, the poet whose meditation is this poem, turns away from the idea of order that every man, and hence every mind, introduces into the life around him, as Stevens himself remarks in his mention of Berkeley. In this sense, the singing ends.[6]

5. Actually what he remembered incorrectly was a phrase in Berkeley's *Three Dialogues between Hylas and Philonous* detached from a sentence condemning Vanini, Hobbes, and Spinoza for what he calls their "miserable refuges . . . in an eternal succession of unthinking causes and effects, or in a fortuitous concourse of atoms." See Berkeley, "Three Dialogues between Hylas and Philonous," in vol. 2 of *The Works of George Berkeley, Bishop of Cloyne*, ed. A. A. Luce and T. E. Jessop (London: Nelson, 1949), p. 213.

6. In this stanza, the voice of the poem addresses an observer of the singer. "Ramon Fernandez was not intended to be anyone at all," Stevens wrote. "I chose two everyday Spanish names. I knew of Ramon Fernandez, the critic, and had read some of his criticisms but I did not have him in mind" (*L*, 798). I trust Stevens' veracity and can find no evidence that would lead me to doubt his plain statement.

He then turns his attention to the "fortuitous concourse of personal orders," which is the complex general or social order and is symbolized by the lights of the fishing boats that "mastered the night and portioned out the sea."

Stevens may have referred to the final stanza when he wrote for the dust jacket of the trade edition of *Ideas of Order* that the poems of that book were concerned with such ideas as "the idea of order created by individual concepts, as of the poet, in 'The Idea of Order at Key West.'" This final stanza is Stevens' hymn to the ardor of the poet to give order to the world by his command of language. Words are portals to thought, this stanza may imply, to thoughts on the nature of man and the origins of consciousness. The passion of the poet for the order that is poetry commits him to its finer discriminations of language—"ghostlier demarcations, keener sounds." It is noticeable that Stevens draws on the schema in this stanza, for the poet's ardent desire to give order to reality is "the maker's rage to order words of the sea."

V

"I am not at home by the sea; my fancy is not at all marine, so to speak." The entry in Stevens' journal for August 24, 1902, shows a preference even at this early date for contemplation over immediacy. "The sea is loveliest far in the abstract when the imagination can feed upon the idea of it" (*L*, 59). The sea in the abstract (to recount the several conceptions of it in the schema) includes the idea of reality in flux and a portent of disintegration; the idea of the natural world and the parent of man; the idea of a physical reality beside and yet apart from the human mind.

This last conception of the sea is that of the first section of "The Woman That Had More Babies Than That." There it is plainly described as "the universal machine" and thus is an image

of the material flux.[7] "An acrobat on the border of the sea"
regards the meaningless repetition of waves as "the merely revolving wheel." Characterization of the figure by the sea as an acrobat
implies that any conception of reality is an act of skill. He considers that this continual mechanical process needs an enrichment
of human realization, with all the thought or "thesis" and feeling
or "music" involved in an experience of the world:

> The acrobat observed
> The universal machine. There he perceived
> The need for a thesis, a music constant to move.   (*OP*, 82)

Stevens apparently felt that there is a reciprocity between mind
and reality, in that the material world needs human thought and
feeling and human conceptions need contact with reality. The
latter idea is presented in the beautiful poem on the MacCullough
in "Notes toward a Supreme Fiction," when it is conjectured that
this idealized figure might receive from the sea or from poetry
"greater aptitude and apprehension."

There are two schemata in this poem. Not only is MacCullough
the figure on the shore, but before that he is considered a figure in
the sky:

> The pensive giant prone in violet space
> May be the MacCullough, an expedient,
>
> Logos and logic, crystal hypothesis,
> Incipit and a form to speak the word
> And every latent double in the word.   (*CP*, 387)

To understand the significance of these two views of the MacCullough and the nature of the MacCullough himself, it is necessary to
turn to Stevens' elliptical explanations of this poem. First he

---

7. Santayana calls the flux of the natural world "the machine of nature"
in *Realms of Being* (New York: Scribner's, 1942), p. 156.

dispels any notion that this figure refers to a particular name or person. The MacCullough is what he is, a fictive person to stand for the idea of man elevated by humanism to take the place of deity. This is the reason for showing the MacCullough in the sky. "The gist of this poem is that the MacCullough is MacCullough; MacCullough is any name, any man. The trouble with humanism is that man as God remains man" (*L*, 434).

In the second schema, Stevens places the MacCullough by the sea—"drowned in its washes"—to indicate how this imagined figure might be modified by immersion in the reality of the world. The poem conjectures that from this contact with reality, or by virtue of the "deepened speech" of poetry, or by recognition of a more modest image of man, this figure by the sea might achieve such an enhancement of capability and understanding that it would be for him as though reality and expression had finally attained the perfection that is the ideal and essence of art:

If MacCullough himself lay lounging by the sea,

Drowned in its washes, reading in the sound,
About the thinker of the first idea,
He might take habit, whether from wave or phrase,

Or power of the wave, or deepened speech,
Or a leaner being, moving in on him,
Of greater aptitude and apprehension,

As if the waves at last were never broken,
As if the language suddenly, with ease,
Said things it had laboriously spoken.   (*CP*, 387)

The exquisite poignancy of the concluding stanza lies in the qualifying phrase, "as if," for the qualification implies that the wave is always broken and the thoughts of poetry, the things it says, are not easily achieved.

Stevens' letter explaining the MacCullough, as quoted above, continues with a few words about the "leaner being" in the next-to-the-last stanza: "But there is an extension of man, the leaner being, in fiction, a possibly more than human human, a composite human. The act of recognizing him is the act of this leaner being moving in on us." And in another letter on the same poem, Stevens discusses the weakness of humanism, as he sees it, by concluding: "The chief defect of humanism is that it concerns human beings. Between humanism and something else, it might be possible to create an acceptable fiction" (*L*, 449). The "acceptable fiction" can be conjectured as the MacCullough modified by the "leaner being."

According to the poem, the MacCullough is "major man," and further elucidation of this figure rests upon what Stevens says about major man. A few years after "Notes toward a Supreme Fiction" Stevens wrote "Paisant Chronicle" in part to define in poetry the idea of major man:

> The major men—
> That is different. They are characters beyond
> Reality, composed thereof. They are
> The fictive man created out of men.   (*CP*, 335)

Stevens explains in a letter that the "major men" of "Repetitions of a Young Captain" are simply men who act heroically in war, "but major men as characters in humanism are different. Since humanism is not enough, it is necessary to piece out its characters fictively" (*L*, 489). However, what he does say in "Paisant Chronicle" about the fictive figure of major man, seen as though he were real man in all his quotidian humanity, is pertinent to an understanding of "the leaner being":

> . . . But see him for yourself,
> The fictive man. He may be seated in

A café. There may be a dish of country cheese
And a pineapple on the table. It must be so.   (*CP,* 335)

Major man in this scene is acceptable because, although fictive, he seems more like a real man than an idealized figure. This is what Stevens means by "the leaner being" moving in on the MacCullough—leaner because it is a more modest conception. As Stevens says, a leaner being is "a possibly more than human human, a composite human" or one that may be more human, more believable, like a character in fiction, than even a real person in all the eccentricity of true individuality.[8]

The schema that shows MacCullough, conceived in the world of place and process, of sea and wave, reclining on the verge of ocean is a scene that suggests ease and accord with the natural world. Harmony with that world is also implied by a similar scene in "An

---

8. When the poet's comments on the MacCullough, major man, and the leaner being are related to one another and to the context of the poem, then what the poem says about MacCullough lounging by the sea can be paraphrased as follows: if an idealized conception of man, like that of humanism, is modified by a more realistic version (the leaner being), one resembling those in believable fictions, then that conception will be more in accord with the natural world and more capable of the arts of man.

Immediately after finishing "Notes toward a Supreme Fiction," Stevens wrote to Henry Church: "About Nietzsche: I haven't read him since I was a young man. My interest in the hero, major man, the giant, has nothing to do with the Biermensch; in fact, I throw knives at the hero, etc." (*L,* 409). Stevens sometimes contradicts himself. For instance, each comment on the MacCullough associates this figure with the idea of man in humanism, and the poem itself identifies the MacCullough as a version of major man; yet only two years after the letters on the MacCullough, Stevens writes that "the major men, about whom you ask, are neither exponents of humanism nor Nietzschean shadows" (*L,* 485). Since this book is concerned with what Stevens has to say about his poetry, I accept his plain statement about Nietzsche at face value. Soon after "Notes toward a Supreme Fiction," Stevens was looking for copies of the works of Nietzsche.

Ordinary Evening in New Haven," XXVII, where two figures lie beside the sea:

> . . . He has thought it out, he thinks it out,
> As he has been and is and, with the Queen
> Of Fact, lies at his ease beside the sea.   (*CP*, 485)

The primary figure here is the "Ruler of Reality" who "rules what is unreal," a personfication of mind ruling over its conceptions of reality. Mind is an illumination rising upon the world, and hence "sunrise is his garment's hem." The Queen of Fact personifies occurrence and phenomena. Events and substances are obscure, except when brightened by the light of attention, and thus sunset is her garment's hem. She rules what cannot be known in itself because fact is something outside of mind. He rules what is abstract—the interior realm of thoughts and images.

Consonance of self and reality is also indicated by the schema of "The Poem that Took the Place of a Mountain," for the sea is characterized here as the "unique and solitary home" of the individual self. The entire poem, schema and all, is recounted by the poet himself as he remembers the experience of conceiving his poem and realizes its special significance for him. In that memory, he is the figure on a shore. "The Poem that Took the Place of a Mountain" is based on a trope that presents poetry as a kind of created point of survey or place—"He breathed its oxygen"—as a mountain overlooking the sea. His book of poems, lying "in the dust of his table," recalls the act of creation:

> It reminded him how he had needed
> A place to go to in his own direction,
>
> How he had recomposed the pines,
> Shifted the rocks and picked his way among clouds,
>
> For the outlook that would be right,
> Where he would be complete in an unexplained completion:

The exact rock where his inexactnesses
Would discover, at last, the view toward which they had edged,

Where he could lie and, gazing down at the sea,
Recognize his unique and solitary home.   (*CP*, 512)

Like so many figurative ideas of Stevens, a version of the trope in
this poem appears in philosophic literature. Santayana imagines
that for a philosopher, the mountaintop of skepticism could provide a view from which to select a dialectical home, for pure
skepticism "may afford, like a mountain-top, a good point of
view in clear weather from which to map the land and choose a
habitation."[9] In similar fashion, Stevens imagines that a poem,
like a mountaintop, provides a point of view from which to ob-
serve the sea of reality and recognize the place and time of one's
own circumstance—unique because experience is always singular
and particular, solitary because that is the essence of individuality.

This occurrence of the schema, like each of the others, presents
a distinct variation of the basic design of the schema and its implication that mind exists on the edge of the reality it observes. It is
when all its recurrences are considered together that the essence
of the schema emerges from the analogy implicit in the scene: a
vision of a solitary figure on the edge of a sea that is a succession
of moments, each of which, as Santayana says, is "one wave in a
sea that is nothing but waves."[10] Thus the schema becomes a representation of someone regarding time and place, a configuration of

9. George Santayana, *Skepticism and Animal Faith* (New York: Dover,
1955), p. 108. Stevens felt a relationship between the imagery of philosophy
and that of poetry. "There is, then, the same rise and fall of images in philosophy that there is in poetry. In the genealogy of representation there is the
same eminent antiquity that there is in any other genealogy, at one end of the
line, and the same restless, impatient, undisciplined fidgetting, at the other
end" (*WS*, 50).

10. Santayana, *Realms of Being*, p. 254.

the nearness and separateness of mind and world. An idea of this kind is openly stated without its depiction by a schema in "The Ultimate Poem is Abstract":

> . . . It would be enough
> If we were ever, just once, at the middle, fixed
> In This Beautiful World Of Ours and not as now,
>
> Helplessly at the edge, . . .   (*CP*, 430)

Six

IT MUST CHANGE

I

Ideally, the letters of a poet should tell enough about the writing of poems to account for changes in the development of his art. During the period of development of Stevens' later style, the 1930s and 1940s, his letters reveal more about his poetry than do those of any other decade. Few, if any, major figures have been as willing as he to try to recall a train of thought at the inception of a poem, to search memory for the significance of figures and symbols, or to examine his changing ideas of the nature of poetry. Stevens' letters, however, create some difficulties for his readers. In the midst of apparently frank explanations, reticence appears, substitutes the occasion or origin of a symbol for its import, clothes definition in the symbolic language of the poems, reduces exegesis to mere paraphrase. Stevens explained his reticence in the course of his correspondence with Latimer:

"As soon as people are perfectly sure of a poem they are just as likely as not to have no further interest in it; it loses whatever potency it had" (*L, 294*).

In spite of these difficulties, Stevens' literary correspondence contains enough information to indicate the kind of factors that must have influenced the development of his poetry. In general, the letters suggest that, like most factors shaping the evolution of an art, those that induce the famous mutation after *Harmonium* are mainly subjective: ideas of excellence, habits in thinking, self-criticism. The shift in his style seems to be concurrent with a change in his conception of his art and to be conformable to his declared growing tendency toward abstraction. The shift in style seems also to be influenced by inductive modes of thinking disclosed during his exposition of the meaning of lines and images.

The most obvious of the guiding factors in the development of Stevens' art is his changing idea of the nature of poetry.[1] When involved with *Harmonium,* he was, he said, an advocate of "pure poetry," in accordance with the notion of the ideal nature of poetry current in the early years of the century. Recalling his conception of poetry of that day, Stevens remarked that "when HARMONIUM was in the making there was a time when I liked the idea of images and images alone, or images and the music of verse together. I then believed in *pure poetry,* as it was called" (*L, 288*). In 1928, answering several questions about *Harmonium,* he regretted whatever adulteration by thought there might be in "Domination of Black." To read it sensuously, he contended, was to read it appropriately. "I am sorry that a poem of this sort has to contain any ideas at all, because its sole purpose is to fill the mind with the images & sounds that it contains" (*L, 251*).

---

1. Stevens disclosed that theory elicited practice. Brushing aside a question about his theory of literature, he said: "One has a theory for each poem; I dare say that, in the long run, they all fit together" (*L, 320*).

In spite of the poet's expressed intention, "Domination of Black" fills the mind with ideas that recur many times in the books after *Harmonium,* for the inner theme of the poem seems to be the resemblances the mind finds in its cohesive work with the natural world, and its intuition of the ultimate resemblance among leaves, fires, stars, everything—their common and eventual extinction. Ideas like these were at least sometimes tacit in the early poems, even those preliminary to *Harmonium.* But in the 1920s, ideas were considered extraneous to the real work of the poem. In the succeeding decade and during the years of the reissue of *Harmonium* and the publication of *Ideas of Order,* thought was rediscovered in poetry. Stevens was already busy with "Owl's Clover," very much aware of the abstract element in his writing and the dangers implicit in abstraction. "A good many people think that I am didactic," he wrote Latimer. "My own idea about it is that my real danger is not didacticism, but abstraction, and abstraction looks very much like didacticism" (*L,* 302). Poetry cannot altogether dispense with thought, he continued, illustrating his point with an image borrowed from Santayana, rather than the better known one from Yeats: "It cannot be made suddenly to drop all its rags and stand out naked, fully disclosed" (*L,* 303).[2]

This realization of his tendency toward abstraction was accompanied by an awareness of a change in his idea of the nature of poetry. "My conception of what I think a poet should be and do changes, and I hope, constantly grows" (*L,* 289). By 1942, he recognized the shift that had occurred in notions of what was appropriate for poetry. "As a matter of fact," he wrote, "the conception of poetry itself has changed and is changing every day"

2. Santayana's version of the image appeared in 1923, when *Skepticism and Animal Faith* was first published. See pp. 71–72 in the reprint (New York: Dover, 1955).

(*L,* 414). By 1943, his correspondence with Hi Simons was well under way and Stevens was committed to a recognition of the place of ideas in his poetry, as well as engaged in defining those ideas for Simons. At the time, Stevens was advising Henry Church about the *Mesures* lectures at Princeton, one of which was Robert Penn Warren's "Pure and Impure Poetry."[3] Warren's essay was an indication of the revolution that had occurred since the Imagists had banished ideas, since George Moore's anthology of pure poetry maintained that thought seeped into poetry only as an adulteration.[4]

Warren traced the history of the term "pure poetry" and demonstrated that it meant different things to different people. During the thirties, Stevens was developing his own understanding of the term, based on his idea that poetry in its real purity—"the poetry of the subject," to use his phrase—was the ground of feeling underlying and giving tone, color, and individual character to the content of a poem, to its conception or meaning. In "The Irrational Element in Poetry," he differentiated between what he called "the true subject" and "the poetry of the subject." From his account, it would appear that "the true subject" is the idea, an element of thought implicit in the poem, and "the poetry of the subject" is the essence of the poem, its inherently imaginative vision, its concentration of feeling, the tone and quality of its language. This essay clearly revealed that his notion of a pure

3. First published in the *Kenyon Review,* spring 1943.
4. Joseph Riddel in *The Clairvoyant Eye* (Baton Rouge: Louisiana State University Press, 1965), discusses some of Stevens' special uses of the term "pure poetry." He not only quotes from "The Irrational Element in Poetry" but also from a statement by Stevens that appeared on the dust jacket of *Ideas of Order.* Stevens speaks of the poems in this book as being void of any economic, political, or social theory and hence as "pure poetry." However, he did describe the ideas of two of the poems—ideas that were incipiently philosophical.

poetry already admitted the presence of ideas. Eventually he wrote "A Collect of Philosophy" to explain that poetry could be inherent in idea just as much as in image and incident.

Stevens' conception of his art changed slowly during the post-*Harmonium* period and progressed rapidly after the second edition of *Harmonium* in 1931. During the thirties, exegesis of his own poems became more frequent in his letters. Discussions of his poems for his correspondents were mostly statements of the nature of the ideas implied in the passages and images that he was asked to explain. By 1942 and the long exegetical letters to Hi Simons, Stevens had become interested in the ideas that his poems might be said to express, even those hidden in the "images and sounds" of *Harmonium*. During the forties, his earlier reluctance to explicate his poems must have largely vanished. He wrote Delmore Schwartz that "the interest in the analysis and interpretation of poetry is the same thing as an interest in poetry itself" (*L*, 590–91).

Shortly before he wrote "Notes toward a Supreme Fiction," his correspondence revealed that he was already considering the dual nature of a poem. He wrote Hi Simons that a poem was like a man in motion casting a shadow into a receiving mind: "a poem is like a man walking on the bank of a river, whose shadow is reflected in the water."[5] The physical man was compared to the actual poem

5. The image of a reflection or shadow was very much in Stevens' mind at this time (1940), for the next year "Poem with Rhythms" appeared in *Parts of a World*. In the poem, the mind casts a shadow in space that is the conception of the world for a man sitting enclosed in a room, or the shadow is the thought and feeling of a woman waiting for her beloved:

The mind between this light or that and space,
(This man in a room with an image of the world,
That woman waiting for the man she loves,)
Grows large against space:

There the man sees the image clearly at last.
There the woman receives her lover into her heart
And weeps on his breast, though he never comes.   (*CP*, 245)

as written or printed; the river to the receiving consciousness; the moving shadow to the poem become thought and feeling in the experience of reading it.

This image of the actual poem that cast a shadow into the mind of the reader was a version of a philosophic metaphor that compared the actual to a body and any idea of it to its shadow.[6] Stevens used the figure to explain his present recognition of the importance of critical interpretation. Now he felt that to point to the poem on the page was insufficient. Explanation of a poem should include its potentialities for a reader. "If you explain a poem, you are quite likely to do it either in terms of the man or in terms of the shadow, but you have to explain it in terms of the whole. When I said recently that a poem was what was on a page, it seems to me now that I was wrong because that is explaining in terms of the man. But the thing and its double always go together" (*L,* 354).

In the 1940s, his willingness to tell whatever he could or should about his own understanding of his poems was still curbed to some extent by the poet's inherent fear of authoritative definitions and set meanings. "I think I said in my last letter to you," he wrote to Hi Simons, "that the Supreme Fiction is not poetry, but I also said that I don't know what it is going to be." Although "Notes toward a Supreme Fiction" had already been published, he seemed to hope that his poem would retain the open character of the creative moment. "Let us think about it," he continued, "and not say that our abstraction is this, that or the other" (*L,* 438).

With his growing willingness to discuss possible and latent meaning in his poems, he also began to conceive that his poems might

6. Bergson distinguished idea from object, in that idea was without weight and mass, "being nothing more than the shadow of a body." *The Creative Mind,* trans. Maybelle L. Andison (New York: Philosophical Library, 1946), p. 167.

be vehicles for abstraction as well as for expression. These two developments seemed to go together because his consideration of and concern for the element of thought in a poem was concurrent with an increasing interest in explicating his poems. It may be that meditation on the abstraction inherent in his own poems—an emphasis that explication itself imposed—led him further into the development of the abstract style so characteristic of the poems he was writing at that time and was to write later.

Passages in two letters illustrate his new conception of his art and show his later willingness to explain poems. In 1928, he declared that "Thirteen Ways of Looking at a Blackbird" was a collection of sensations, not of ideas (*L,* 251). But in 1939, when asked about the same group of poems, he discovered latent ideas within them. Of number XII, he said that "the point is the compulsion frequently back of the things that we do" (*L,* 340). The slight infusion of ideas in the poem depends on the word "must":

> The river is moving.
> The blackbird must be flying.   (*CP,* 94)

The flowing of the river and the flying of the blackbird—activities inherent in the nature of river and bird—suggest that the individual creature is as impelled by the universal flux as is the river, a natural image of the flow of things. The compulsion of the flux is often expressed in the deliberative rhetoric of Stevens' later style, for example, in "Notes toward a Supreme Fiction":

> There was a will to change, a necessitous
> And present way, a presentation, a kind
> Of volatile world, too constant to be denied.   (*CP,* 397)

And later in "An Ordinary Evening in New Haven," the compulsion is that imposed by inevitability:

But he may not. He may not evade his will,
Nor the wills of other men; and he cannot evade
The will of necessity, the will of wills—   (*CP*, 480)

The style of the middle and later periods is a subtle modification of the early manner. The change becomes apparent when a poem or a passage from *Harmonium* is compared to a passage of similar import from one of the later books. Although the later poems retain much of "the gaiety of language" and "the quirks of imagery" of the poems of his first book, the change of style for a reader fresh from *Harmonium* is apparent in both rhetoric and feeling. The later style has an air of explicit theorizing, even though theory is tentative and undeveloped. Undoubtedly the element of thought is brought more to the fore, and tone is somewhat deepened, perhaps because it is the tone of a man intent on his illusions, aware that no matter where he looks he is looking inward, and yet—considering how far outward the mind seems to reach—"outsensing distances."

II

His letters during the years of transition from *Harmonium* to "Notes toward a Supreme Fiction" show that Stevens, even while impelled toward symbolic presentation, never lost his interest in a poetry that expresses the actual, a poetry of specific sights and sounds and sensations. Although the letters were written after the poems under discussion, they reveal the impulses of the poet, his essentially inductive habits of thought, as he considered and reconsidered the nature of the figures of his poems. Trying to recall the significance of these figures, he hesitated between person and personification. And usually, while he considered their significance, specific things and people became instances of universals. "One often symbolizes unconsciously," he wrote Hi Simons in explanation of the planter of "Notes toward a Supreme Fiction." Then, bringing his image into conscious attention, he concluded: "I suppose that it is possible to say that the planter is a symbol of change." Reflecting inductively in this way, he expanded the significance of the planter into a paradigm of the life of each man: "He is, however, the laborious human who lives in illusions and who, after all the great illusions have left him, still clings to one that pierces him" (*L*, 435).

The discussions of the images in the poems disclose that his tendency toward abstraction is a tendency to think in terms of synechdoche, for the planter is not only the kind of man he is but also an example of the total of human lives, an instance of the whole or universal of which he is a part. Stevens, at times, was reluctant to reveal the whole or the universal he implied. He knew that poetry must exist for what it was in itself, and even though a poem contained the seeds of abstraction, of a hypothetical extension of thought beyond its stated meaning, he insisted that it run its own immediate course of language and sensibility. "A poem of symbols exists for itself. You do not pierce an actor's make-up: you go to see and enjoy the make-up; you do not bother about the face beneath. The poem is the poem, not its paraphrase" (*L*, 362).

The comments in the letters show that Stevens, even while disavowing symbolic presentation, invokes ideas by means of images. In his exposition of the figures of men in his poems, these figures, while he explains them, take on the character of universals, become the symbols he rejects at first. His remarks on the nature and meaning of the men and women of the poems disclose a bent toward the inductive mode of thought, a propensity that must have affected the character of the development of his poetry. Discussing the significance of Canon Aspirin in "Notes toward a Supreme Fiction," he remarked that "Canon Aspirin is simply a figure, not a symbol. This name is supposed to suggest the kind of a person he is" (*L*, 427). Later, in another letter, the Canon was described as "the sophisticated man . . . who has explored all the projections of the mind, his own particularly" (*L*, 445). The Canon returned from all these explorations of his imagination to the innocent mind of his sister, who lived only in the "sensible ecstasy" of daily practical existence; for Canon Aspirin, Stevens said, had never acquired "a sufficing fiction."

The discussion of Canon Aspirin was expressed in purely secular terms, and the relationship of the clerical figure with the religious imagination was carefully avoided. At the end of his comment, Stevens could not resist this amused hint: "How he ever became a Canon is the real problem" (*L*, 445). The problem was solved by the inductive action of synecdoche. In describing the "kind of person he is," Stevens shows him as representative of a certain kind of thinking. The Canon expands into a figure representing the traditional and sophisticated thought of the history of theology. As for the name Aspirin, Stevens assured his correspondent that it had no literary source. Quite likely, Canon Aspirin's name was an ironic suggestion that the orthodox religious imagination could be a comfort for human limitation and mortality.

The many figures that appear momentarily in the poetry of Stevens, like the Arabian or the dead shepherd of "Notes toward a Supreme Fiction," develop as universal ideas by means of the internal logic of the poem itself. The dead shepherd, Stevens explained in a letter to Simons, emerged out of the beginning of the poem, "A lasting visage in a lasting bush," and its idea that man projects the human face of deity upon the natural world (*L*, 438). The idea of deity so conceived finally becomes outworn. It might be that the idea of deity is "too venerably used," the poem continues, or it "might have been" (casting the idea into the past). But a particular idea of deity eventually becomes myth:

> . . . But as it was,
> A dead shepherd brought tremendous chords from hell
>
> And bade the sheep carouse.   (*CP*, 400)

The dead shepherd is an orphic figure whose music ("tremendous chords") creates feeling and colors existence even after he ceases to be a person and has become only a personified idea. He seems to be the music (in Stevens' usual sense of music) of mythology. "This dead shepherd was an improvisation," Stevens remarked, but he quickly qualified the statement by insisting that the improvisation was a natural development and not an irrelevancy, without purpose. "What preceded it in the poem made it necessary, like music that evolves for internal reasons and not with reference to an external program" (*L*, 438). Perhaps Stevens indicated by this statement that he intended no allusion to a specific religion or mythology. Instead, he utilized the traditional orphic figure but did not purpose an allusion to Orpheus, away from the poem to the myth itself.

Stevens usually avoided specific allusion and created out of the universal figures descriptive sketches of persons like the mother and father in "The Auroras of Autumn," or the lover and beloved (Ozymandias and Nanzio Nunzio) in "Notes toward a Supreme Fiction." He gave these figures symbolic significance by means of his own set of recurrent connotations. Sometimes he seems to have felt that the inner logic of the poem gave sufficient significance to a figure and offered its own explanation. "The Arabian," Stevens wrote to Simons, referring to the third poem of "Notes toward a Supreme Fiction," "is the moon; the undecipherable vagueness of the moonlight is the unscrawled fores: the unformed handwriting." Later he added: "The fact that the Arabian is the moon is something that the reader could not possibly know. However, I did not think that it was necessary for him to know" (*L*, 433–34). Stevens apparently felt that the Arabian, by the character of the image itself, would suggest man's speculative imagination. He did not feel that it was necessary to mention the moon, his symbol of the imagination, to bring out the significance of an image that could be understood by means of its presentation within the poem itself.

This third poem of "Notes toward a Supreme Fiction" illustrates Stevens' use of the reasoning within a poem to set forth the meaning of its imagery. The poem divides, like a sonnet, into two parts. The first four stanzas describe the power of poetry as intuition in that, like intuition, it gives to the world of the poem the freshness and the verity or "candor" of things first conceived. The intuitive power of poetry (according to the implications of this poem) arises from the animal basis of consciousness—from "thought/Beating in the heart." The second part begins with "we say," and what "we say" is an illustration of the thesis set forth in the first part:

> We say: At night an Arabian in my room,
> With his damned hoobla-hoobla-hoobla-how,
> Inscribes a primitive astronomy
>
> Across the unscrawled fores the future casts
> And throws his stars around the floor. By day
> The wood-dove used to chant his hoobla-hoo
>
> And still the grossest iridescence of ocean
> Howls hoo and rises and howls hoo and falls.
> Life's nonsense pierces us with strange relation.   (CP, 383)

Those stanzas present several layers of nonsense. "Arabian," "wood-dove," and "ocean" have an utterance that is basically the same, differing only in a scale that grows more elaborate, from the sound of water, its "hoo," to the sound of thought, its "hoobla-hoobla-hoobla-how." The Arabian becomes in the poem an embodiment of the imagination, in accordance with the usual symbolic significance of the moon in Stevens' work, as mentioned in the letter and defined by the reasoning in the poem. As the human speculative imagination, the Arabian makes his predictions with arbitrary fortuitous conjectures, like an astrologer casting horoscopes, scattering his stars around the floor. The utterance of the Arabian is the nonsense of conscious intelligence; that of the wood-dove is instinctive babble; and that of the sea is the fortuitous noise of substance in motion. An inference from this series might be that human conjecture is irrational, like instinct or reflex, and meaningless, like the automatic action of simple materiality. All are no more than spontaneous sounds of the natural world.

The poem illustrates the characteristics of the later style, the aphoristic air, the discursive tone, the theoretical implications, the suggestion of logical form—all expressed in the light figurative language that is Stevens' unmistakable signature. Concurrently, Stevens' inductive habits of thought can be seen at work in the expansion of the wood-dove and the Arabian into the universals, the abstractions he said he could not avoid. These habits of thought illustrated here were important factors in determining the characteristics of the style of this period.

III

The poem as a unique, ideocratic, effectual composition, a complete expression in itself of what it is—this was the concept of Stevens' art developed during the 1940s. One letter in 1945 set forth his idea of poetry of that period, an idea consonant with the character of many of the poems in *Transport to Summer* and *The Auroras of Autumn*. He explained that his purpose in writing was to create the singular thing that was the poem. The element of thought could be dense or tenuous, but, in any case, was only an element of the composition. "However, a poem must have a peculiarity," he said, "as if it was the momentarily complete idiom of that which prompts it, even if that which prompts it is the vaguest emotion" (*L,* 500). What prompted the poem may have been an idea, or, as he said, "the vaguest emotion." It may have been only a faint sense of place called up by a letter from a friend; there are many kinds of meditations, and ideas are not their only subject.

The meditation that prepared "Attempt to Discover Life," for instance, must have been occasioned by an evocation of a scene characteristic of the poet's feeling for the Cuban milieu. The place existed for him in a casual phrase that he quoted from a letter of his Cuban correspondent, José Rodríguez Feo: "It was at dusk that I arrived from San Miguel de los Baños and tore the carefully packed package and in an atmosphere of roses and yellow and Uccello blues I peruse the book" (_L,_ 528). (Rodríguez Feo was thanking Stevens for a copy of the Cummington Press edition of _Esthétique du Mal._) "Attempt to Discover Life," in its opening lines, presented a scene that apparently came to mind in response to the place name and the roses of the letter:

> At San Miguel de los Baños,
> The waitress heaped up black Hermosas
> In the magnificence of a volcano.
> Round them she spilled the roses
> Of the place, blue and green, both streaked.   (_CP,_ 370)

Hermosas were a variety of rose, Stevens explained to his Cuban friend, and even if they did not grow in Matanzas province, the San Miguel of the poem was, he said, "a spiritual not a physical place" (_L,_ 540).

According to Stevens' idea of such things, spiritual means imagined, abstract, conceived. The scene of the poem is a table set for the pleasure of the company, one of several symbolic tables in Stevens, the specific of time and place for the serving or occurrence of whatever may come to exist. The profusion of roses expands into the profusion of nature: "The blue petals became/The yellowing fomentations of effulgence." Coming to the table are the archetypal man and woman. The Cuban milieu is reflected in their appearance. The Latin characterization of the woman is especially vivid, for Stevens usually made the image of woman the essence of the world he envisioned:

A woman brilliant and pallid-skinned,
Of fiery eyes and long thin arms.
She stood with him at the table,
Smiling and wetting her lips
In the heavy air.   (*CP*, 370)

The two figures vanish and in their place the tip may be seen:

On the table near which they stood
Two coins were lying—dos centavos.   (*CP*, 370)

In the same letter, he stated that the point of the conclusion was a question: "whether the experience of life is in the end worth more than tuppence: dos centavos" (*L*, 540). The question was answered by the tip left on the table. But one cannot be sure of the character of the answer, for the irony of the conclusion is part of its ambiguity. However, the point, the idea, was not what the poem achieved, not even its essential "meaning."

Speaking of another poem, he said "the point of that poem is not its meaning." The statement is from a 1945 letter and suggests the kind of concept of poetry that he had developed by that date (*L*, 500–501). Although he could assert that "supreme poetry can be produced only on the highest possible level of the cognitive," at the same time he had his own notion of the "special manner of thinking in poetry." In this letter, he described "the special thinking of poetry" as intense realization. Poetry, therefore, reached toward a fulfillment of an essential human need, and in his eyes, was profoundly important. "It is simply the desire to contain the world wholly within one's own perception of it."

IV

"Criticism," Stevens said, "is disturbing, whether it is favorable or unfavorable." For that reason he seldom read it, he maintained

(*L*, 484). According to the evidence of his letters, he did read his critics; they did disturb him, in time invaded his own conception of poetry, and thus modified the trend of his development. Although his critics were in general complimentary, in later years even adulatory, for a while there was a tendency to see his work as remote from the real world and its real conditions. There is speculation that this kind of condescension toward *Harmonium* was to some degree responsible for his long silence after 1923 (*L*, 242). When that book first appeared, critics found it fastidious, finely wrought, exquisitely trivial—"one of the jewel boxes of contemporary verse." "Well Moused, Lion" was the deprecatory title of Marianne Moore's commendatory review. Sensitive as he admittedly was to criticism, Stevens must have discerned in these early reviews a suggestion that he was fanciful and his poetry artificial. When he resumed writing in the 1930s, he apparently wished to show that he was deeply concerned with the reality of the world. He began to revise his notion of what his poetry should express and considered that he might "try to make poetry out of commonplaces: the day's news; and that surely is owl's clover" (*L*, 311).

For "The Old Woman and the Statue," the first poem of "Owl's Clover," he looked back to a period long before *Harmonium* and to an early experience with a poetry of poverty and distress. As an undergraduate he had written a group of "Street Songs," one poem of which was an expression of a sense of wretched humanity and triumphant art. "The Beggar" is a description of an old woman whose poverty is her misery: "She asks with her dry, withered hand of dreg/Of the world's riches" (*Buttel*, 32). To some degree, the image and the idea of indigence and art of "The Old Woman and the Statue" had been used in the early poem. "The Beggar" contrasts wretchedness and art, the old woman and the cathedral where she begs, and her distress, her indigence, to the carvings and beauty of the cathedral. The poem begins: "Yet in this morn there is a darkest night," and that night is the black-ness of misery that makes the beggar oblivious to the work of art, the cathedral. In her dark mood, "fancy is a thing that soothes—and lies,/And leads on with mirages of light." The "mirages of light" anticipate "the light fell falsely" of "The Old Woman and the Statue" (*OP*, 44). The "darkest night" of the beggar's misery and the beggar's mind becomes in the later poem "a mind in a night" and "a night that was that mind" with a similar import.

The next poem of "Street Songs," called "Statuary," describes the idea of art as independent and impending form and feeling; men wonder at its jubilance and are never blind to its presence. The statue in the early poem is "Dian and Apollo"; it stands for the idea of art in a world indifferent to that idea, as does the statue of winged horses of "The Old Woman and the Statue." The essence of the two poems, "The Beggar" and "Statuary," dormant in his mind for many years, could very well have ger-minated and developed, even without conscious recollection, into integration for "The Old Woman and the Statue."

This first poem of "Owl's Clover" was an attempt to give, he said, "the effect of the depression on the interest in art. I wanted a confronting of the world as it had been imagined in art and as it was then in fact" (*OP*, 219). The whole of "Owl's Clover" was in this respect a departure from his earlier desire to write pure poetry. He seems to have been influenced to some extent by a tendency in some critics to insinuate that his work did not repre-sent the contemporary mind and its contemporary problems.

Stevens' response in the uncut version of the second poem of *Owl's Clover* to Stanley Burnshaw's well-known review of *Ideas of Order* was a reaction to ideas, as Joseph Riddel said, rather than a reply to a person.[7] However, the fact that Stevens did respond, and in verse, is evidence of his considerable sensitivity.

7. Joseph Riddel, *The Clairvoyant Eye*, p. 289.

When *Owl's Clover* itself was reviewed, Stevens willingly acknowledged his difficulty, in view of his temperament and talent for exuberant and elliptical expression, in reaching toward "order and certitude" by formal discourse, "a difficulty that I have long been conscious of and with which I am constantly struggling." However, what seemed to disturb him was the old intimation that his poetry was essentially decorative. "What I tried to do in OWL'S CLOVER was to dip aspects of the contemporaneous in the poetic," Stevens wrote one of his critics. "You seem to think that I have produced a lot of Easter eggs, and perhaps I have" (*L*, 314).

Although his new intentions may have been induced by the spirit of the age as much as by the condescension of his critics, nevertheless he began his next long poem with an air of contention:

> They said, "You have a blue guitar,
> You do not play things are they are."
>
> The man replied, "Things as they are
> Are changed upon the blue guitar."   (*CP*, 165)

In the first half dozen poems of "The Man with the Blue Guitar," the poet seems to be justifying his highly individual poetry. It is a justification without rancor and more in the mode of persuasion than of refutation. Except for a letter to Fred B. Millett (*L*, 319–20), all of Stevens' responses to critics, whether direct or indirect, give an impression of a wish to mollify rather than to oppose. Evidently he thought reviews that could be favorable might increase public acceptance of his work. "Looking at them wholly from my own point of view, their value is in bringing about a certain amount of acceptance. People never read poetry well until they have accepted it" (*L*, 436).

In spite of the commendation of some of the best critical minds of that period, Stevens suffered during the 1930s from the derogation of a few Marxist critics like Geoffrey Grigson, who wrote of him as "observing nothing, single artificer of his own world of mannerism" and, to make the charge of unreality even more specific, as "describing thirteen ways of seeing a blackbird, forgetting the blackbird."[8] It was the general imputation that his poetry offered none of the reality of things that Stevens seemed to answer the year after he saw Grigson's review of *Ideas of Order*:

> I cannot bring a world quite round,
> Although I patch it as I can. (*CP*, 165)

Grigson's review had the opprobrious title, "The Stuffed Goldfinch." Within two years, Stevens recommended Grigson's *New Verse* as "the best poetry magazine" and said Grigson "has his eye on the right values" (*L*, 332).

Whatever the cause, "The Man with the Blue Guitar" represented a definite change in Stevens' manner. The subdued tone, the reasonable voice, the simplicity of sentence and wording, the pervasive modulation—all this was the beginning of a phase in his work that culminated in "An Ordinary Evening in New Haven." It was during this time—the late 1930s and early 1940s—that Stevens considered the relative merits of what he called the normal or central, as compared to the irrational or marginal. In 1935, he observed: "I never feel that I am in the area of poetry until I am a little off the normal" (*L*, 287). Five years later, he wrote Hi Simons that formerly he took his stance as a poet apart from the normal, as though on the edge, but now he wished to be in the center, to share the common life. "People say that I live in a world of my own: that sort of thing. Instead of seeking therefore for a

8. Quoted by Samuel French Morse in *Wallace Stevens: Poetry as Life,* pp. 149–50. This is an excellent estimate of the pressure brought to bear on Stevens by his critics.

'relentless contact,' I have been interested in what might be described as an attempt to achieve the normal, the central." Stevens told Simons that knowing this "may be useful to you in understanding some of the later things" (*L*, 352). Stevens' willingness to change his idea of what his poetry should express, to meet the objections of critics who felt that he lived in a world of his own, is also useful "in understanding some of the later things."

A glance at the table of contents for *Parts of a World* or *Transport to Summer* reveals the nature of his "attempt to achieve the normal, the central." There are, for instance, "The Man on the Dump," "On the Road Home," "The House Was Quiet and the World Was Calm," "A Woman Sings a Song for a Soldier Come Home." Along with the scattering of poems reflecting the daily circumstances of normal living, there are many others that indicate Stevens' continued interest in abstraction, with the unusual scenes and persons that often embody his ideas. Not long before he finished *Transport to Summer,* he wrote Henry Church: "For myself, the inaccessible jewel is the normal and all of life, in poetry, is the difficult pursuit of just that" (*L*, 521).

This is the spirit in which he wrote, for instance, "A Lot of People Bathing in a Stream." Primarily, the poem seems to be a memory of the normal human experience it professes to describe. The feeling of immersion in water and light and color, the sense of space and flow—all immediate, almost subliminal experiences—dominate the account:

> It was like passing a boundary to dive
> Into the sun-filled water, brightly leafed
> And limbed and lighted out from bank to bank.   (*CP*, 371)

In the faint plot of this poem, the poet has had a vivid experience and then returned to accustomed surroundings, to his rooms "which do not ever seem to change." The unchanging rooms, in contrast to the flowing stream, bring to mind another dimension of the poem. In accordance with the symbolic sun and river of other poems, "the sun-filled water" can be assumed to be the flux of physical reality. The people immersed in the stream are "floating without a head," for in this water they live below the level of reflection, in both senses of the word. Since they are no more than "anonymids" or "less/Than creatures," they appear to be presented in a purely physical state, mere bodies in the flux—"the water flowing in the flow of space." Until the last stanza, the poem is concerned with amorphous organic life, "gulping for shape among the reeds" and submerged in the time-space continuum.

The conclusion of the poem turns to the structured life of the consciousness and its familiar, cognizable scenes or concepts—for example, "the frame of the house" and its rooms that "do not ever seem to change." The known, the constituted, gives an illusion of permanence, the security we feel while we prepare for bed, as the poem indicates. This preparation for sleep carries very lightly its connotation for mortality and the irony of that connotation:

How good it was at home again at night
To prepare for bed, in the frame of the house, and move
Round the rooms, which do not ever seem to change.

(*CP*, 372)

A poem like this discloses the fact that, in his pursuit of the normal, Stevens never really altered the basic character of his symbolic meditations on the human condition. In fact, his considerations of man's existence, even if not always associated with the normal, were for him certainly the central. The real effect of his later intentions in poetry were a modulation of tone and language and of the settings of his meditations.

While the normal was still the center that he sought, he continued to talk of his interest in a poetry dominated by a sense of ordinary reality. In 1944, he maintained that "the things that I have written recently are intended to express an agreement with reality" (*L*, 463). This was said in some irritation because of an impression he had formed of Yvor Winters' famous essay, "Wallace Stevens, or the Hedonist's Progress." He refused to read Winters' book at that time, but, from what the reviews said, concluded it denigrated his poems as expressions of "Paterian hedonism." The phrase must have recalled early critics of his work like Paul Rosenfeld, who condemned his "characteristic note of 1890" and spoke of his "archness and comic pudicity as slightly timed."[9]

An immediate response to unsympathetic criticism is quite naturally defensive. But a generous spirit like Stevens would eventually consider this kind of criticism objectively. In fact, he once remarked that adverse criticism "always does one more good than the highly favorable kind of thing" (*L*, 529). In time, he began to accommodate to a degree his own conception of poetry to that of some unsympathetic critics. A characteristic of Stevens' mind was its tendency to adopt first one and then another contrary point of view. Although he never truly changed the genre that was native to him, he did gradually modify its rhetoric. Eventually he seems to have been affected by conceptions of his work like that of Julian Symons, who, while granting Stevens technical mastery, said, nevertheless, that his subject was trivial, his language flippant, and his poems, however readable, "a fribble of taste."[10] By 1946, Stevens said the misery of Europe had affected him so deeply that his poems recently published in *Origines* seemed to him "academic and unreal. One is inclined, therefore, to sympathize with one's more unsympathetic critics" (*L*, 525).

Three years later, he was at work on "An Ordinary Evening in

9. "Wallace Stevens," in *The Achievement of Wallace Stevens,* ed. Ashley Brown and Robert S. Haller (Philadelphia: Lippincott, 1962), p. 40.

10. Brown and Haller, *The Achievement of Wallace Stevens,* p. 122.

New Haven''; he explained that his intention in this poem was "to try to get as close to the ordinary, the commonplace and the ugly as it is possible for a poet to get." The explanation was an answer—although certainly it would never have occurred to him that it was an answer—to the critics who had found beneath the magnificence of his poetry something that was "academic and unreal," to use his own harsh words. "The object is of course," and he seems now to be speaking to his own spirit of self-criticism, "to purge oneself of anything false" (*L*, 636).[11]

Perhaps his response to those who had spoken of his technical skill, his mastery of the traditional poetic rhetoric, and who saw it all turned to the service of the fanciful or of "Paterian hedonism" was this desire for a conjunction of poetry and reality. Still echoing the idea of his art that had dominated the writing of "An Ordinary Evening in New Haven," he wrote in 1951: "Isn't it the function of every poet, instead of repeating what has been said before, however skillfully he may be able to do that, to take his station in the midst of the circumstances in which people actually live and to endeavor to give them, as well as himself, the poetry that they need in those very circumstances?" (*L*, 711). Poems written under the aegis of such a conception still reflected his individuality, but with a rhetoric and a tone adapted to this view of his art and of himself. One poem says that the "plain sense of things" comes to us in late autumn or in old age, as the poem figuratively indicates:

> After the leaves have fallen, we return
> To a plain sense of things. It is as if
> We had come to an end of the imagination.   (*CP*, 502)

11. Stevens, however, had no intention of writing for anyone except himself: "I think that I should continue to write poetry whether or not anybody ever saw it, and certainly I write lots of it that nobody ever sees" (*L*, 306).

Yet, as he says, the plain sense of things is itself an imaginative act, even though it may seem to lack a visionary or poetic perspective:

> Yet the absence of the imagination had
> Itself to be imagined. The great pond,
> The plain sense of it, without reflections, leaves,
> Mud, water like dirty glass, expressing silence
>
> Of a sort, silence of a rat come out to see,
> The great pond and its waste of the lilies, all this
> Had to be imagined as an inevitable knowledge,
> Required, as a necessity requires.   (*CP*, 503)

The great pond is an image of the phenomenal world as it seems to one with a desire for a conjunction of poetry and plain reality. The waste of the lilies represents the prodigality of nature, a proliferation of forms emerging and vanishing. The rat is the simple perceptual consciousness with a plain sense of things, neither expressing nor conceiving, silently and without purpose looking, looking at the scene of its life—the pond, its debris of leaves and mud, and its lilies.

Poems like this one are essentially of the meditative, symbolic genre that Stevens had always made his own. His poetry was not at all diverted from its tendency toward philosophical implications, and it continued to hold its abstract discourse while endeavoring, by its rhetoric, to come to an accord with his professed desire to hold "an agreement with reality." Stevens never intended to write a poetry of psychological or sociological realism, not even one of realistic description. "Nothing in the world is deader then yesterday's political (or realistic) poetry," he wrote Barbara Church in these later years. "Nevertheless the desire to combine the two things, poetry and reality, is a constant desire" (*L*, 760). This desire began to become apparent in the 1930s, and it influenced the tone and settings of the later poems, especially those of the last two decades of his life. The desire seems to have begun in part as a delayed unconscious response to early criticism.

Yet, if he was sometimes, as he said, inclined to sympathize with unsympathetic criticism, his susceptibility neither improved nor reduced the quality of his poetry. To know that he valued his first book as well as the last, that he recognized the great poems in each as well as the uniquely interesting lesser ones, it is enough to look at the choices he once made for a selected poems, the English edition, or to remember that he preferred to call the body of his work "the whole of *Harmonium.*"

Seven

 # THE STYLE AND THE POEM
WERE ONE

I

"I am rather inclined to disregard form so long as I am free and can express myself freely," Stevens said in reply to a question about technique. "I don't know of anything, respecting form, that makes much difference" (*L,* 323). External form, the restraints of conventional verse structure, was the kind of form he disregarded. Although he might in this way denigrate imposed regularity, he created his own kind of formal symmetry.[1]

1. An example of skillful use of stanzaic form to support the meaning of a poem is Stevens' great elegy in a country churchyard, "Dutch Graves in Bucks County." This poem offers a contrast between the stillness of the dead and the chaotic strife of the living. The couplets addressed to the dead alternate with five-line stanzas that describe the living. Stevens' use of external forms like his frequent three-line stanzas has been described by many critics. This study is limited to notes on some of the forms assumed internally by the meanings of his poems.

Form in its vital sense was for Stevens semantic form—arrangements of meaning significant for the poem as a total composition. "Poetic form in its proper sense," he explained in a statement for the *Partisan Review*, "is a question of what appears within the poem itself" (*L*, 590). What he seems to indicate as the proper sense of form is the order that results from the organization of the poet's thought for the purpose of expression.

Speaking from the viewpoint of the art of making a poem, he said that "poetry and painting alike create through composition" (*NA*, 163). Earlier, Stevens had described, in his elliptical fashion, the part composition plays in the making of poems. He indicated that as a poem develops in the poet's mind, a pattern of meaning takes shape, then becomes definite and intricate, and when his thought has arranged itself, the intensity engendered by emerging form releases the poet's inventive flow of language. His statement was an explanation of the source of sudden verbal inventiveness: "I suppose that the explanation for the bursts of freedom is nothing more than this: that when one is thinking one's way the pattern becomes small and complex, but when one has reached a point and finds it possible to move emotionally one goes ahead rapidly" (*L*, 297).

Stevens believed that to create by composition, the poet needed an energizing factor that would offer a basis for the composition.[2] The one that he favored was the interaction of two concepts, like the ideas of art and human misery in "The Old Woman and the Statue." In a context that related interaction of various kinds, especially between two elements, he wrote that "Cross-reflections, modifications, counter-balances, complements, giving and taking

2. To illustrate the idea that for poets and painters alike, an interaction of elements was a principle of composition, he quoted from an article on Seurat: "In the comparison of aesthetic opposites (lines at right angles, complementary colors, etc.) and the slight divergences of likenesses, he sees the source of all artistic beauty" (*L*, 369).

are illimitable" (*L,* 368–69). Probably the majority of his poems are constructed of various interrelationships like these. Near the end of his career, he was convinced that the interplay of two or more concepts engendered poetry. "Interaction is the source of poetry," he affirmed (*OP,* 293–94).

His interest in the interaction of two concepts extended to his appreciation of effects gained this way in the work of other poets—what he called "cross-fertilization" or "hybridization" when speaking of Eliot (*OP,* 252). In a review of a collection of William Carlos Williams' poetry, he remarked that its essential component was often "the constant interaction of two opposites" (*OP,* 256).

"Dry Loaf" is an example of a poem in which internal form is an arrangement of an interaction of two themes. Stevens' prose note for the last page of *Parts of a World,* the book in which "Dry Loaf" appeared, states two concepts that seem to be the same themes used in "Dry Loaf": "The immense poetry of war and the poetry of a work of the imagination are two different things" (*PEM,* 206). The poetry of war, Stevens says, is its immense fact, and he suggests that this fact invades the imagination. In the poem, the imagination is represented by a painting and the fact of war by images of marching soldiers and of human misery. To introduce the two themes, the poem begins with an aphoristic generalization that equates living in a tragic time, a time of war, with living in a tragic place, a landscape the poet says he is painting behind the dry loaf of the title:

> It is equal to living in a tragic land
> To live in a tragic time.
> Regard now the sloping, mountainous rocks
> And the river that batters its way over stones,
> Regard the hovels of those that live in this land.
>
> That was what I painted behind the loaf,

The rocks not even touched by snow,
The pines along the river and the dry men blown
Brown as the bread, thinking of birds
Flying from burning countries and brown sand shores.

(*CP*, 199–200)

The loaf in the foreground is an image of the idea of bare sus-
tenance for the continuance of life and in that sense suggests
want and necessity. In this landscape, the mountainous rocks are
possible symbols of the fundamental reality or ground of existence. Other symbolic possibilities are the river flowing for time
continually passing, the hovels for a poverty of human existence
in this tragic place, the dry men for the aridity of human feeling,
the birds migrating "as if the sky was a current that bore them
along" for the idea of inevitability. As these objects are observed
in this way, the painting becomes something meditated rather
than visualized.

The poem then turns from its first theme, a work of the imagination, to its second theme, the immense fact of war and the tragic
time, which is the equivalent of the tragic place for one living
then:

It was the battering of drums I heard
It was hunger, it was the hungry that cried
And the waves, the waves were soldiers moving,
Marching and marching in a tragic time
Below me, on the asphalt, under the trees.   (*CP*, 200)

In the final stanza, the poet, who has alternated his two themes,
combines them by introducing the soldiers into the painting and
the birds of the painting into the reality of asphalt and martial
parades. The interaction suggests the idea of Stevens' prose piece
on the poetry of war: not only is the painting a tragic one as a result of the fact of war that influences the tone of the imagination,

but the fact of war also enters the creative work of the artist. The birds from the painting have a symbolic effect on the tragic time because they are a representation of the inevitability of events for the soldiers and for the hungry—the birds had to migrate, the soldiers had to march:

> It was soldiers went marching over the rocks
> And still the birds came, came in watery flocks,
> Because it was spring and the birds had to come.
> No doubt that soldiers had to be marching
> And that drums had to be rolling, rolling, rolling.   (CP, 200)

An element of many of Stevens' poems that is in a sense an element of semantic form is a kind of detached image, almost an insert, that sets forth as symbol or by connotation the feeling or theme or major concept of the poem. This is the function of the image of the dry loaf: to serve as an emblem of the poem's sense of the poverty of life in a time of war. An image that seems to be almost a foreign element in the poem's discourse—one that is of a different category than the other images and is presented abruptly or occurs in a kind of isolation, yet is linked to the poem by its symbolic function—will be called an emblem in these notes on interior form.

Often the emblem stands at the conclusion of a poem—for instance, the image that depicts the idea of the poem at the end of "Burghers of Petty Death." The semantic form of this poem presents in alternation its two themes: first the idea of individual death as that of the man and the woman on whose grave the grass is still green and who still cling like two dead leaves not yet swept away by the blast of winter from the autumnal tree of life, and second the idea of a universal of death, its black cold of total obliteration:

> Of great height and depth
> Without any feeling, an imperium of quiet,

In which a wasted figure, with an instrument,
Propounds blank final music. (*CP*, 362)

The emblem of this poem, the wasted figure playing an instrument, is a version of Stevens' favorite schema. At the same time, it is a monument of absolute desolation "covering all surfaces,/ Filling the mind."

II

Overall, the semantic form of a poem by Stevens seems to be a development of thought toward disclosure that remains a possibility. Meaning impels anticipation through successive statements, with an intent whose consummation is its closure. The semantic form of a Stevens poem is most often this progression toward an appearance of persuasion, celebration, explanation, or revelation. In an ultimate sense, every poem has its own individual interior form. Stevens probably looked at his arrangement of meaning within a poem in this light when he said in a note on Paul Rosenfeld, that "this constant shaping, as distinguished from constancy of shape, is characteristic of the poet" (*OP*, 262–63). By shaping, he must have intended arranging. In poems, shapes are truly semantic forms or patterns of meaning. Some arrangements are obvious; the subtlety of others escapes most analysis. All are important to the individuality of a poem.

Stevens' typical arrangement of meaning, like the alternation of two themes or a dual theme presented and then repeated in a series of variations, are inherent in the nature of his theory of interaction. There must have been a preconceived pattern for the more complex ones like "The Hermitage at the Centre," with its two poems entwined as one, for the first line of each stanza read continuously makes one poem and the remaining lines of each stanza make another. A simpler Stevens device is the use of the same or similar phrases at the beginning and end of a poem. This kind of repetition becomes functional when it has the delicacy of a variation or echo and is incorporated into the poem's interior arrangement. The faint echoing, at the conclusion of a poem, of phrases resembling those at the beginning can give the poem's inner form a lyric roundness. This is the function of such echoing in "Woman Looking at a Vase of Flowers." Near the opening of the poem is its major statement:

> . . . the crude
> And jealous grandeurs of sun and sky
> Scattered themselves in the garden.   (*CP*, 246)

True to the seeming of perception, these lines and their variation at the close explain the transformations of light into color and space into form, as though they were occurring externally, in the world of things, instead of internally, in realization:

> The crude and jealous formlessness
> Became the form and the fragrance of things
> Without clairvoyance, close to her.   (*CP*, 247)

Some echoings are so interwoven into the pattern of thought of a poem that they are an essential element of its semantic form. Intricate semantic forms involving such echoings, as well as other arrangements, may have been what Stevens had in mind when he said that "the inclination toward arbitrary or schematic constructions in poetry is, from the point of view of style, very strong; and certainly if these constructions were effective it would be true that the style and the poem were one" (*OP*, 205). Perhaps semantic form is arbitrary or open to choice until the poet has thought his way into it. Then it becomes a schematic structure and formative of the final development of the poem.

One poem that has the appearance of arbitrary and schematic construction is "World without Peculiarity." Its overall form is that of an interlacing of positive and negative concepts of earth. The first line or two of each of the first three stanzas expresses the positive concept as an enjoyment of the beauty of the natural world: the strength of the day, the silent movement of the moon, the spiced air of summer. The remainder of each of these stanzas recounts the negative concept as an awareness of mortality or sadness or hostility: of the father lying in his grave, of sorrow for the dead mother, of the antagonism of the beloved:

> The day is great and strong—
> But his father was strong, that lies now
> In the poverty of dirt.
>
> Nothing could be more hushed than the way
> The moon moves toward the night.
> But what his mother was returns and cries on his breast.
>
> The red ripeness of round leaves is thick
> With the spices of red summer.
> But she that he loved turns cold at his light touch.
>
> (*CP*, 453)

The symbolic quality inherent in the images of day and father, moon and mother, summer and beloved, are latent but possible. The overt meaning is the primary one of real father, mother, beloved. In the last three stanzas, the poem turns its attention to the archetypal earth mother. As "the fateful mother," she assumes her negative aspect.[3] In her beneficent aspect she is, as the poems says, humanity itself, thus implying that the earth mother has an identity only in human experience. When man thinks of

---

3. The earliest mention of the negative concept of earth appeared in a letter of 1907 as "Nature, this cruel mother" (*L*, 100). The latest was "Madame La Fleurie" in 1951. In between were many poems that celebrated earth as the beloved.

his mortality and conceives of earth as "the fateful mother," he is an "inhuman son" as regards his concept of the archetypal mother. Then he does not know her, for earth is known only in immediate experience.

The pattern of this poem becomes apparent in the last two stanzas, where the positive aspects of the earth mother—the day, the movement or "walk" of the moon, the spices of summer— are repeated from the first three stanzas. The negative concepts recur in the last stanza in like manner: the poverty of dirt in which his father lies, the oppression on his breast that is his sorrow for his mother, the antagonism of the beloved or "the hating woman." And from the fifth stanza, the idea of earth that he does not know recurs in this negative listing as "the meaningless place":

> He is the inhuman son and she,
> She is the fateful mother, whom he does not know.
>
> She is the day, the walk of the moon
> Among the breathless spices and, sometimes,
> He, too, is human and difference disappears
> And the poverty of dirt, the thing upon his breast,
> The hating woman, the meaningless place,
> Become a single being, sure and true.   (CP, 454)

When man is engaged in the bodily, given over to his senses, the world is without peculiarity; "difference disappears" if the mind abandons thought for absorption in immediate experience. Then all aspects, negative and positive, are merged into the one being of his apperceptive unity, for, as Stevens says in the "Adagia," "The world is myself" (OP, 172).

In the middle of the poem, the poet interrupts the pattern of alternate concepts to speak of his own feeling, rather than reflect on the circumstance of the imagined person of the poem. He expostulates against any idea that he should assuage his sense of mortality with the knowledge that he is a part of enduring earth. The passage seems to be a reply to Schopenhauer (one of several in Stevens' work).[4] "Now, since man is Nature itself, and indeed Nature at the highest grade of its self-consciousness, but Nature is only the objectified will to live, the man who has comprehended and retained this point of view may well console himself, when contemplating his own death and that of his friends, by turning his eyes to the immortal life of Nature, which he himself is."[5] Stevens' elliptical and bitter query implies a denial of Schopenhauer's justification of mortality:

> What good is it that the earth is justified,
> That it is complete, that it is an end,
> That in itself it is enough?
>
> It is the earth itself that is humanity . . . (*CP,* 453–54)

The stanza of expostulation, although not an image, has all the other characteristics of an emblem. It is an insert and not integrated into the poem's flow of discourse. It seems instead to epitomize the sense of mortality latent in the whole poem, like an aside from the poem's alternating conceptions of the earth mother.

III

Stevens often spoke of his deep interest in "the theory of poetry" and by that phrase he did not mean, he says, an *Ars*

4. Discussion of Stevens' poetry in relation to Schopenhauer's thought can be found in my book, *Stevens' Poetry of Thought*; in Richard A. Macksey's "The Climates of Wallace Stevens," in *The Act of the Mind,* ed. Roy Harvey Pearce and J. Hillis Miller (Baltimore: Johns Hopkins Press, 1965); and in Richard P. Adams' "Wallace Stevens and Schopenhauer's *The World as Will and Idea,*" *Tulane Studies in English* 20 (1972): 135–68.

5. *The World as Will and Idea,* trans. R. B. Haldane and J. Kemp (Garden City, N.Y.: Doubleday, 1961), p. 288.

Poetica. "I mean poetry itself, the naked poem, the imagination manifesting itself in its domination of words" (*NA,* viii). "Things of August," III is a poem concerned with the imagination manifesting itself in two ways in its domination of words. The poem speaks of high and low poetry, but figuratively, and not as though one were superior to the other. This calm and beautiful poem has a functional semantic form based on Stevens' usual alternation of two concepts. The overall form is that of an increase, a growth, and must have been one of his arbitrary or schematic constructions.

The poem starts with simple naming: "High poetry and low." Then each definition of these terms is an enlargement of the poet's conception of these two experiences of poetry. Thus the semantic form is an expansion from its beginning to its conclusion and may illustrate the growth of a poem in the poet's mind. The alternation of the two concepts is a possible representation of the poet's experience of a collaboration of the two faculties indicated by perihelion and penumbra. High poetry is closest to the sun that is the peak of conscious creativity; low poetry is the light of creativity on the edge of the subconscious:[6]

> High poetry and low:
> Experience in perihelion
> Or in the penumbra of summer night—   (*CP,* 490)

The second and then the third (or last) stanza each describes how high or low poetry appears to the poet as he is writing. At the peak of consciousness, it seems to the poet that he hears his sen-

---

6. A rudiment of the idea of high and low poetry occurs in "An Ordinary Evening in New Haven," XVII, lines 8 through 15. High poetry is "the high serious" and is described as a garment woven of a pattern of meanings and decorated with tropes. Low poetry, introduced by "or," the conjunction that indicates alternation, is "the wasted figurations of the wastes/Of night, time and the imagination" (*CP,* 477).

tences "like interior intonations," for this is the illusion that goes with an awareness of wording as it comes to the poet:

> The solemn sentences,
> Like interior intonations,
> The speech of truth in its true solitude,
> A nature that is created in what it says,
> The peace of the last intelligence; ...   (*CP*, 490)

The first line of the last stanza, "Or the same thing without desire," describes the experience of spontaneous inventiveness, of the poem that seems to write itself. The poet exists in the world of his words as though in the external world of phenomena—"a world of objects," and by the living imaginative quality of that world of words—"being green and blue"—he feels the quiet happiness of effortless achievement:

> Or the same thing without desire,
> He that in this intelligence
> Mistakes it for a world of objects,
> Which, being green and blue, appease him,
> By chance, or happy chance, or happiness,
> According to his thought, in the Mediterranean
> Of the quiet of the middle of the night,
> With the broken statues standing on the shore.   (*CP*, 491)

Poetry that seems to come without an effort of will, to be realized by happenstance, arises from the interior sea that is the subconscious (to use the term favored by Stevens)—"Mediterranean" because it is within his earth, his body, and at night because of the obscurity of the subconscious. This image of the midnight sea, with its ruins on the shore like those of the antique world, is the poem's emblem—an unexpected image, unlike the other imagery of the poem. The emblem suddenly presents a glimpse of the nature of creativity. The broken statues themselves

are symbols of memories, fragments of old experiences still standing but on the verge of oblivion. The poetry of summer night is influenced by these fragments of his past life of experience.

Soon after the writing of "Things of August," Stevens indicated
that upon completion of a group of poems, other poems would
come to him from something left over: "As usual, I now want to
go on under the impulse of ideas that occurred to me but which I
did not use, and I do in fact intend to go on" (*L,* 685). This sort
of thrust brought the image of the broken statue as memory to
further development in the second part of "Two Illustrations
That the World Is What You Make of It."

The subtitle, "The World Is Larger in Summer," refers to the
difference in vividness and scope between remembered and immediate experience. The marble pieces in the grass are remnants
of a luminous moment now past:

> He left half a shoulder and half a head
> To recognize him in after time.
>
> These marbles lay weathering in the grass
> When the summer was over, when the change
>
> Of summer and of the sun, the life
> Of summer and of the sun, were gone.   (*CP,* 514)

The marble pieces symbolize his memory of a moment of intuition—the whole man who was the totality of that experience, as
though in sculpture. Like the ruin of an antique statue from an age
of fullness of being, portions of the experience are all that is left:
"half a shoulder and half a head." The experience itself was an intense realization of a tree as a living thing apart—a spruce glittering
in its separate being, yet suffused in the blue light that is a subjective vision of it:

> He discovered the colors of the moon
>
> In a single spruce, when suddenly,
> The tree stood dazzling in the air.   (*CP,* 514)

The conclusion of this radiant poem compares the one who sees the spruce to a forgotten artist—"the master of the spruce":

> The master of the spruce, himself,
> Became transformed. But his mastery
>
> Left only the fragments found in the grass,
> From his project, as finally magnified.   (*CP*, 515)

The master of the spruce, like an unknown early painter, is identified by his subject matter; thus the moment of intuition is comparable to a painting, it is implied. And this realization, this painting, was a project of the master of the spruce when in the totality of that moment the project was, according to the poem, "fully magnified." It is another way of saying "the world is larger in summer," for an intuition fully lives in the poised moment of present physical existence.

There is a generalization early in the poem, almost an aphorism of the kind usually placed by Stevens near the beginning of a poem; the generalization states that a change occurs in both perceiver and thing perceived when that thing is realized:[7]

> He had said that everything possessed
> The power to transform itself, or else,
>
> And what meant more, to be transformed.   (*CP*, 514)

Then follows the instance that illustrates the generalization: the moment of intuition. In many of his poems, generalization followed by instance gives the poetry its semblance of logic.

The semantic form of this poem has an element that is figurative in itself—a symbolic possibility. The image of the broken statue is placed at the beginning and end of the poem. Thus the

---

7. This notion is expressed in a letter of 1916 about his play, "Carlos Among the Candles." "The play is simply intended to demonstrate that just as objects in nature offset us . . . so, on the other hand, we affect objects in nature, by projecting our moods, emotions, etc." (*L*, 195).

fragments of the self of a former time hold the remembered moment as in an enclosure, seeming to symbolize the idea that memory holds portions of experience from the past. As this enclosure,
this imagery at first and last, seems placed there for symbolic
purposes and is separate by character and function from the rest
of the poem, it serves as the poem's emblem.

IV

The poems of *Harmonium* had their own kind of internal form,
and, as Stevens looked back at some of them, about twenty years
after the book's publication, he commented on their structure of
repetition and varied pace of meaning. Of "Sea Surface Full of
Clouds"—one of the more obvious constructs, based on an arrangement of theme and variation—he wrote that "it is obvious that the
repetition of a theme and the long-drawn-out rhythm that results
from the repetition are merely mechanisms" (*L*, 390).

Several years later, he speculated that "The Curtains in the
House of the Metaphysician" was written "at a time when I felt
strongly that poems were things in themselves," and he wrote of
"long motions—part of the structure of the poem, which is a poem
of long open sounds" (*L*, 463). The movement of thought in this
poem is the basis of its semantic form; the pattern moves but
stays, in accordance with the succession of clauses that are similes
for the "long motions" of the curtains:

>   . . . as the ponderous
> Deflations of distance; or as clouds
> Inseparable from their afternoons; . . .   (*CP*, 62)

And continues to:

>   . . . all motion
> Is beyond us, as the firmament,

Up-rising and down-falling, bares
The last largeness, bold to see.   (*CP*, 62)

He seems to have felt a certain stasis in these phrases, for as he
turned to comment on "The Place of the Solitaires," he began,
"On the other hand" and described it as "a poem actually in motion: in motion with the activity of thought in solitude" (*L*, 463).

Stevens' letters show a history of some recurrent dissatisfaction
with the poetry he had written, often a temporary disparagement
of poems later favored. In gathering poems together for *Harmonium*, he said they made him wish to be as obscure a person as
possible "until I have perfected an authentic and fluent speech
for myself." The poems were "outmoded and debilitated," he felt
(*L*, 231).

It may have been in a kindred mood that he wrote the charming
poem that begins "In the land of the peacocks, the prince thereof"
(omitted from *Harmonium*).[8] In this anecdote, the land of the
peacocks is the realm of the imagination, and its prince is a poet
tired of the romantic, in a pejorative sense of the word. Perhaps it
is the prince's own poetry that he is "pondering," as his interjec-
tion ("the deuce!") would suggest. And it is possible that Stevens
projected his own feelings into these lines:

In the land of the peacocks, the prince thereof,
Grown weary of romantics, walked alone,
In the first of evening, pondering.

"The deuce!" he cried.

8. This poem does not seem to me to be an early version of "Anecdote
of the Prince of Peacocks." The two poems differ in meaning, imagery, and
tone. What they have in common is insufficient to conjecture that the weaker
poem developed into the other. Perhaps it was a companion poem. The two
could have been originally intended to be a set.

And by him, in the bushes, he espied
A white philosopher.
The white one sighed—

He seemed to seek replies,
From nothingness, to all his sighs.   (*PEM*, 402)

Although the philosopher, like a skeptic, seems to look to nothingness for answers, unlike a skeptic, he speaks in an "outmoded and debilitated" style that the prince eschews. The philosopher is, apparently, under a compulsion because he smothers his lips, and the prince's shudder is also spontaneous:

"My sighs are pulses in a dreamer's death!"
Explained the white one, smothering his lips.

The prince's frisson reached his fingers' tips.   (*PEM*, 402)

The prince's idea of the romantic was defined by Stevens a number of years later: "the romantic in the pejorative sense merely connotes obsolescence" (*OP*, 251). "Sailing after Lunch," a poem of the period following the 1931 edition of *Harmonium*, reflected the mood of a poet weary of what for him has become an outworn style, and Stevens showed that he was still pondering the matter after two years. "As a man becomes familiar with his own poetry, it becomes as obsolete for himself as for anyone else. From this it follows that one of the motives in writing is renewal" (*OP*, 220).

The poet of "Sailing after Lunch" seeks renewal in a new kind of romantic. The title is a trope for writing poetry in the afternoon of life, and the creative act here is a sail on the lake. The historical sail through the mustiest blue is one that represents writing poetry in the style of the romantic that "must never remain," the old romantic. To get under way, the poet must turn to a new romantic that is the living, "the enriching poetic reality"

(*OP*, 253). This is largely a matter of feeling, the poem says: "Where my spirit is I am." To get under way, one must expunge "what people speak of as the romantic" (*L*, 277). Then the poet must become a student of reality, a pupil of the symbolic sun— "the gorgeous wheel":

> To expunge all people and be a pupil
> Of the gorgeous wheel and so to give
> That slight transcendence to the dirty sail,
> By light, the way one feels, sharp white,
> And then rush brightly through the summer air.   (*CP*, 120)

Stevens indicates that this poem is about the effect of a change of feeling and attitude. What takes on transcendence in the poem is "the dirty sail," the poet's style, which had been soiled by frequent use. "Without this new romantic, one gets nowhere; with it, the most casual things take on transcendence" (*L*, 277). A year or two later, he identified style with its most casual aspects. "The slightest sound matters. The most momentary rhythm matters." (*OP*, 226).

According to the poem, the poet's style takes on transcendence "by light," thus suggesting the idea of the sun, the reality that he must "study." Stevens explains the rush through the summer air, the "sharp white": "And the poet rushes brightly, and so on. What one is always doing is keeping the romantic pure: eliminating from it what people speak of as the romantic."[9] The elimination of obsolescence and the study of "the gorgeous wheel" of reality would enable him to achieve a renewal that would bring about a poetry in a new style.

---

9. For a thorough investigation of Stevens' concept of "romantic," see A. Walton Litz, "Wallace Stevens' Defense of Poetry: *La poésie pure,* the New Romantic, and the Pressure of Reality," in *Romantic and Modern,* ed. George Bornstein (Pittsburgh: University of Pittsburgh Press, 1977).

However, the later style of an older poet is never quite a new one. Stevens' inventive genius, displayed in the luxuriance of *Harmonium*, appears to have evolved into a variety of styles. But to read the comparatively spare rhetoric of "The Man with the Blue Guitar" and the flamboyant language of "Owl's Clover," both published in one book, is to realize that we are hearing the same voice.

The later poems are more aphoristic than those of his first book, and the tone more chastened.[10] From *Parts of a World* on, the imagery is less profuse in relation to the more frequent assertions, and the lyricism is subdued. The anecdotal approach to idea becomes more expository. While granting Stevens rhetorical virtuosity, it can be said that he did have a later style with certain recognizable characteristics that make a unity of this virtuosity. After all, a characteristic must recur to be recognizable; our sense of style is a sense of repetition within rhetoric.

Style is "not a dress," Stevens affirmed, not an external aspect of a poem. "It may be said to be a voice that is inevitable" (*OP*, 210). The voice can be discerned in the frequent imperatives— "fly low, cock bright, and stop on a bean pole;" in the abundant conditional expressions—"if seeming is description without place"; and in the conjunctions of analogy, with their clauses subordinate in a grammatical sense but dominating by virtue of length and intensity—as in the poem, "Prologues to What Is Possible," for instance. The beginning of poem XVII of "An Ordinary Evening in New Haven" describes the voice of his poetry, and the idea is epitomized in one of the "Adagia" as follows: "Gaiety in poetry is a precious characteristic but it should be a characteristic of diction" (*OP*, 178):

10. The influence of aphorism on Stevens' style is admirably discussed by Beverly Coyle in "An Anchorage of Thought: Defining the Role of Aphorism in Wallace Stevens' Poetry," *PMLA* 91 (1976): 206–22.

The color is almost the color of comedy,
Not quite. It comes to the point and at the point,
It fails. The strength at the centre is serious.   (CP, 477)

This delineation of voice would seem to be especially descriptive of the tone of the *Harmonium* period. He intended that his later work would have the tone described in the final stanza of the poem:

These fitful sayings are, also, of tragedy:
The serious reflection is composed
Neither of comic nor tragic but of commonplace.   (CP, 478)

Tone is the most characteristic element of a poet's style; it is the essence of voice.

After tone, the poet's practice with metaphor is the element that contributes most to what is recognizable in his style. "When you ask about a pattern of metaphors you are asking about the sort of thing with which one constantly experiments" (L, 297). His experiments must have included personification because he personifies almost every abstraction that enters a poem and often builds entire poems on this trope. The last poem of "Notes toward a Supreme Fiction," for instance, is addressed to the "fat girl, terrestrial" that Stevens identifies as earth (L, 426). Another example is "The Owl in the Sarcophagus," with its forms that "move among the dead."[11] A departure from conventional metaphor is his preference for symbolic images, with an implied analogy

---

11. "Forms among the dead" are not versions of the ghost image discussed in the fourth chapter of this book. These forms are personifications of our ideas—"the mythology of modern death" (CP, 435). An admirable explanation of these forms is that of J. Hillis Miller in *The Act of the Mind*, pp. 152–53. His description of the third figure as a personification of "living reality," the present instant, I would extend as the living reality in the continuum of consciousness, the apperceptive unity within the present moment.

rather than the kind of trope that presents both elements in comparison; an example is the broken statue of "Two Illustrations That the World Is What You Make of It."

The most pervasive sentence forms of the later poems perform metaphorical functions. Relationships, interactions, conjunctions—all the aspects of comparison or contrast—are provided by the devices of apposition and predicate nominative. An example of a predicate nominative that creates a metaphor is this comparison of the mind that comforts itself with euphemistic images of death to a child going to sleep with song and pleasant fancies:

> It is a child that sings itself to sleep,
> The mind, among the creatures that it makes.   (*CP*, 436)

Apposition gives the same sense of separateness and identity of two things, except that the commas substitute for the verb to be:

> Jerome and the scrupulous Francis and Sunday women,
> The nurses of the spirit's innocence.   (*CP*, 461)

These two devices say that one image, one concept, one substantive, is equal to another, although by the very statement of equivalence or by the appositive position, it is implied that the equality is really an identity of aspects and a separation of essences, like the relationship in metaphor. In its simple forms, conventional metaphor has the import of a predicate nominative. "Autumn howls upon half-naked summer" (*CP*, 437) contains two conventional metaphors. The first states by implication that autumn is a howling wind; the second implies that late summer is a half-naked woman. Of course, there are other implications, such as the suggestion of the howl of a beast, but the example is sufficient to show the resemblance of the two forms.

These assertions of resemblance that appear to be statements of equalization, or these series of modifications that seem to be reconsiderations, the predicate nominative which says this is that, or the appositive which states that one thing becomes another, another, another—these are the characteristic sentence forms of Stevens' later style.

The special quality of the late style is so permeated with the effects of apposition that some critics have considered that it resembles improvisation, and it may be that often it is. This effect occurs because in apposition the poet seems to deliberate about his original concept. He appears to reconsider it by seeking an equivalent in another and another version, continuously altered yet presented as though it were the same.

Predicate nominative and apposition work together in poetry. "The rock is the gray particular of man's life": "The house is evening, half dissolved"; "The poem is the cry of its occasion"; "The town was a residuum,/A neuter shedding shapes in an absolute"; "The poet is/The angry day-son clanging at its make;/The satisfaction underneath the sense,/The conception sparkling in still obstinate thought"—these are the characteristic sentence forms of the late poetry. Since they express resemblances almost to the point of identification, these grammatical forms express Stevens' sense of reality. "Poetry is a satisfying of the desire for resemblance," Stevens says, and he feels that by resemblance poetry "touches the sense of reality, it enhances the sense of reality, heightens it, intensifies it" (*NA,* 77).

All sorts of conjunctions provide some of the effects of conventional metaphor, but the effects of verbal equations are borne by balances of meaning. There can be no merging of aspects until the possibilities in common meaning between the two concepts are understood, as in these subtle balances of idea: "Description is revelation"; "The eye's plain version is a thing apart"; "words of the world are the life of the world." Looking into the nature of Stevens' verbal equations, we find them to be a certain kind of realization. A realization of this nature is sudden insight into relationship; as such, it can be taken to be a

metaphor, as in this comparison of poetry and the life of the
mind:

> . . . the theory
> Of poetry is the theory of life,
>
> As it is, in the intricate evasions of as,
> In things seen and unseen, created from nothingness,
> The heavens, the hells, the worlds, the longed-for lands.
>
> (*CP*, 486)

The realization here is of the interrelationships of the nature
of poetry and experience. Their use of metaphor "in the intricate evasions of as" is their way of touching reality; of avoiding,
yet meeting unapproachable blank fact by seeking resemblances;
and of understanding one thing in terms of another. These interrelationships extend to reverberations of meaning in poetry and
interpretation in experience ("things seen and unseen"), to the
inventions of poetry and the self, to their conceived aversions,
their longed-for conceptions, their definition of feeling through
idea.

The last poem of "An Ordinary Evening in New Haven" illustrates this idea of a relationship of poetry and realization. It is a
figurative description of the growth of an experience with reality,
and that reality is described in the last line as, perhaps, the act
of experience itself—"a force that traverses a shade." It is also an
account of the growth of a poem in the poet's mind. In this account, the poem originates as heard, barely discernible implications, and as perceptions that are incipient and rarely borne into
consciousness: "The less legible meanings of sounds, the little
reds/Not often realized." Then the first signs of poetic wording
begin to separate from the heavy beat of daily talk: "the lighter
words/In the heavy drum of speech." The poet's intensity in-
creases. His thoughts are hidden within him, shielded from daily

intercourse. The music of his poem is unheard possibility in the general noise of existence. And when the poem emerges, it is as though these beginnings were faint lights snuffed out when the poem appears in consciousness, mere flashes in the motion of the unconscious:

> . . . the inner men
>
> Behind the outer shields, the sheets of music
> In the strokes of thunder, dead candles at the window
> When day comes, fire-foams in the motions of the sea, . . .
>
> (*CP*, 488)

These "Flickings from finikin to fine finikin," the poems says, are the onset of the poem's final realization in statement:

> These are the edgings and inchings of final form,
> The swarming activities of the formulae
> Of statement, directly and indirectly getting at, . . . (*CP*, 488)

Directly "getting" at is exemplified by an image of unconscious creativity, "like an evening evoking the spectrum of violet." Indirectly getting at is illustrated by two figures who practice in order to reach for a perfection.

The concluding stanza supposes that reality is not substance but may be experience. The poem conjectures that reality may be a shade, or shadow, a reflection from the external world falling into the consciousness—itself an insubstantiality and therefore, perhaps, a shade or ghost—that traverses the dust that is man's ultimate essence. Or, the poem further considers, reality may be a force, the life force or will, that traverses that shade or reflection of the world. The traversal is the life that must be lived in the movement of time:

> It is not in the premise that reality
> Is a solid. It may be a shade that traverses
> A dust, a force that traverses a shade. (*CP*, 489)

That the object of the poem being made is to get at reality becomes evident with this last stanza, which appears without a connective, an ellipsis typical of Stevens. When related to the long first sentence that describes the writing of a poem, the conclusion would seem to suggest that reality, as shade or force, is moving in the mind even as that mind acts to write the poem trying to get at reality.

Index of Poems

Index of Names and Titles

The Johns Hopkins University Press
This book was composed in IBM Aldine Roman text and VIP Palatino display
type by Horne Associates, Incorporated, from a design by Susan Bishop. It
was printed and bound by Universal Lithographers, Inc.

Library of Congress Cataloging in Publication Data

Doggett, Frank A.
Wallace Stevens, the making of the poem.

Includes index.
1. Stevens, Wallace, 1879–1955—Criticism and interpretation. I. Title.

PS3537.T4753Z626   811'.5'2   79-22772
ISBN 0-8018-2324-2